Understanding
Multiplication
Across the Grades

Understanding Multiplication Across the Grades

 Mathematics Education Collaborative (MEC)
Under the Leadership of Ruth E. Parker

HEINEMANN · PORTSMOUTH, NH

Heinemann

A division of Reed Elsevier Inc.

361 Hanover Street

Portsmouth, NH 03801–3912

www.heinemann.com

Offices and agents throughout the world

The authors and publisher wish to thank those who have generously given permission to reprint borrowed material:

Figure 1 from *Adding It Up: Helping Children Learn Mathematics*. Copyright © 2001 by the National Academy of Sciences. Reprinted with permission of the National Academies Press, Washington, D.C.

 This project was supported, in part, by the National Science Foundation. Opinions expressed are those of the authors and are not necessarily those of the Foundation.

Library of Congress Cataloging-in-Publication Data

    Understanding multiplication across the grades / Mathematics Education Collaborative, under the leadership of Ruth E. Parker.

        p. cm. — (supporting school mathematics: how to work with parents and the public)

    ISBN 0-325-00937-6 (acid-free paper)

    1. Multiplication—Study and teaching—Activity programs—United States.

2. Mathematics—Study and teaching—Parent participation—United States.   I. Parker, Ruth E.   II. Mathematics Education Collaborative.   III. Series.

QA115.M845 2006

372.7'2—dc22   2005030484

Editor: Victoria Merecki

Production: Lynne Costa

Cover and interior design: Jenny Jensen Greenleaf

Typesetter: Kim Arney Mulcahy

Manufacturing: Steve Bernier

Printed in the United States of America on acid-free paper

10 09 08 07 06 VP 1 2 3 4 5

Contents

Acknowledgments

The six workshop sessions in the *Supporting School Mathematics* series were developed by the Mathematics Education Collaborative's (MEC) Public Session Development Team, a group of mathematics education leaders. Team members include:

Jo Boaler, Mathematics Education, Stanford University

Nicholas Branca, Mathematics Department, San Diego State University

Joan Carlson, Mathematics Educator, Mendocino, California

Sandie Gilliam, Teacher, Scotts Valley, California

Cathy Humphreys, Lecturer, College of Education, Stanford University

Jerry Johnson, MEC Associate and Mathematics Department, Western Washington University, Bellingham

Ellen Lee, MEC Associate, San Diego, California

Patty Lofgren, MEC Associate, Portland, Oregon

Lisa Mesple, Teacher, Boulder Valley School District, Colorado

Ruth Parker, MEC CEO, Ferndale, Washington

Bonnie Tank, Instructional Specialist for Mathematics, San Francisco Unified School District, retired

Special thanks to the Parent Academic Liaison (PALS)/Special Services and the Translation Services/Communications Departments of the San Diego Unified School District for providing Spanish translations of the MEC public sessions.

Getting Started

Purpose of this Session

Understanding Multiplication Across the Grades is designed to help parents learn about how multiplication can be taught for understanding. Parents experience ways to teach multiplication in important and engaging mathematical contexts such as probability, geometry, and data analysis. Fun and engaging ways to provide practice with basic facts are highlighted. The difference between a focus on rote memorization and a focus on knowing and understanding is highlighted. The content of this session is appropriate for teachers and parents of grades 3 through 8, and students of grades 4–8.

Introduction

An informed public is essential if necessary changes in the teaching of mathematics are to occur on a broad scale. Professional organizations such as the National Council of Teachers of Mathematics (NCTM), the National Research Council (NRC), and the Mathematical Sciences Education Board (MSEB) have called for broad and sweeping changes in the mathematics content taught at the K–12 levels, in the learning environment, in the role of the teacher in the mathematics classroom, and in methods of assessing mathematical understandings. Sustained efforts to support teachers and schools in making these changes have been launched on many fronts over the past decade. Sound and comprehensive mathematics programs have been developed. Yet most mathematics reform efforts to date have fallen far short of the vision put forth by the mathematics education community.

One reason increasingly recognized as a contributing factor to this lack of success has been our failure to adequately engage with parents and the public in ways that help them understand important issues in mathematics education, the need for change, and the nature of changes needed. Misinformation about mathematics education is prevalent in today's media. Strategic attempts to organize parents in opposition to reform-based programs are prevalent and are negatively impacting mathematics restructuring efforts taking place in many locations throughout the country. Although the need for working with parents and the public is widely recognized, many teachers and administrators feel inadequately prepared to work with parents in support of quality mathematics programs in their schools.

In response to this need, the Mathematics Education Collaborative (MEC) was founded in 1999 to strategically aid schools and school districts in working with their parents and public in support of quality mathematics programs. Ruth Parker, CEO of MEC, has worked with parents and the public in more than two hundred communities throughout the nation during the past eight years. A National Science Foundation grant (ESI#9908602) has supported MEC's work with parents and the public in three regions of the country during the past five years. The grant also supported the development of *Supporting School Mathematics: How to Work with Parents and the Public*, a series of six interactive sessions designed to help parents and the public understand some fundamental changes that have taken place, or need to take place, in mathematics classrooms. All the sessions have been extensively field-tested by teacher leaders in school districts throughout the nation. The six sessions, which are available separately or as a package, include the following:

◆ *Understanding Addition and Subtraction in the Primary Grades*

◆ *Encouraging Mathematical Thinkers: The Basics and More*

◆ *Understanding Multiplication Across the Grades*

◆ *Understanding Fractions Across the Grades*

◆ *Helping with Math at Home: Ideas for Parents*

◆ *Helping with Math at Home: More Ideas for Parents*

Included with each session is *A Planning Handbook for Presenters*, developed to assist you as you plan and prepare for presenting any and all of the six sessions.

Using the Parent Sessions

These parent sessions are designed to complement the multifaceted work that a school district does to improve mathematics education. They are designed specifically to help parents and the public understand important issues that surround mathematics education today. This series of sessions will help parents learn to recognize quality mathematics programs, support the work of teachers and administrators, and advocate for strong mathematics programs in their schools. These sessions are designed to help teachers and administrators as they prepare to work with parents and the public. The sessions are intended to give parents opportunities to learn about strong mathematics programs. They are set up a little differently than some of the more familiar school math events. It is critical to the sessions that the presenters go beyond the activities and give the audience a chance to think about the issues involved. Each session is based on a few important ideas that are revisited throughout the session. Presenters need to familiarize themselves with these big ideas and use the sessions to help parents understand them. Presenting the sessions as a series of activities without the important discussions, while fun and interesting, will not accomplish the intended goals. It is important to be clear about the main messages in each session and about the mathematical goals.

These sessions are designed to bring about new insights for parents. They have been designed to run between ninety minutes and two hours. They have worked successfully with groups as small as fifteen and as large as one hundred or more. Although participants are actively engaged as learners, the sessions generally require a minimal amount of manipulative materials and technology.

Planning the Sessions

A Planning Handbook for Presenters has been developed to assist you as you plan and prepare for presenting any or all of the six parent sessions. It includes practical advice you will want to consider on topics such as getting parents to come, child care, addressing language needs, and engaging parents during the session. A major part of the handbook addresses questions that parents commonly ask about math in classrooms, along with sample responses. One section of the handbook addresses the issue of invented and alternative algorithms. This section is included because the issue is so central to changes occurring and to the concerns some parents have about elementary mathematics education. You will find that this handbook is also useful when you are developing your own sessions.

Making the Sessions Your Own

It is important for you as a presenter to know the session well and, in as many ways as possible, make it your own. This may mean changing some of the anecdotes and telling your own stories. It may mean using your own student work. It may mean talking about your own experiences in the classroom with students. Using personal examples to illustrate points helps your presentation "ring true" and be more convincing to parents.

Addressing Local Needs

You will need to customize the presentation to address local issues so the audience can connect to the message. For example, find out what textbooks and what assessments are used locally. Try to understand whether and in what direction the district or school is trying to move. Try to anticipate the questions and concerns of the parents. More information about these issues can be found in *A Planning Handbook for Presenters*.

Student Work

Many of the sessions call for the use of student work. Student work is another powerful tool to use in convincing parents about the importance of a strong mathematics program. Yet it is also difficult for a presenter to be knowledgeable about student work when it comes from someone else's classroom. In some sessions, one example of student work is included to show what the assignment might look like, but it is assumed you will collect your own student work to discuss during the session.

Because it is important that you become familiar with the games and/or activities before presenting them to parents, you will want to try them with a group of students first. This will allow you to gather student work and anecdotes for your presentation. It will also familiarize you with questions that come up during the activities and help you troubleshoot the directions. You will then be able to more confidently answer parents' questions about the assignment and the work.

Understanding the Mathematics

Some of the sessions also include a section about the mathematics of the problem presented. The mathematical explanations are included when a problem is apt to be misunderstood. If you are presenting one of these sessions, you will need to explore the mathematics and become comfortable with the theoretical ideas behind the problem. Though you may not need to provide a mathematical explanation during the session, you will want to be prepared to do so in case you are asked by parents about the mathematics of the problem.

Adapting the Sessions to Use with Teachers

The content of these sessions is also very appropriate for teachers and administrators who are learning more about mathematics education. The sessions can be easily adapted to use for professional development by reviewing the session ahead of time and changing some of the language that is used; for instance, use *participant* or *teacher* rather than *parent*. In addition, the focus of the session and the issues addressed may need to be slightly modified for teachers. You might want to choose more appropriate quotes that have more meaning for the classroom. It is a good idea to go through the entire session considering your specific audience and make adjustments where necessary.

Research

Many times parents have questions about the research that exists on a particular mathematical issue. There is a user-friendly and useful research-based overview of the issues in the document *Teaching and Learning Mathematics: Using Research to Shift from the "Yesterday" Mind to the "Tomorrow" Mind*. It was written by Dr. Jerry Johnson and can be found at the following website: www.k12.wa.us. A free copy of the document can be obtained by placing an order on the website or by calling 888-595-3276. You can choose to use information from this source for your presentation or give parents access to the document itself. Another resource for current articles about mathematics education is www.mathematicallysane.com. You may also want to start your own collection of articles that you think will be useful for parents to read and discuss.

Other Resources

Included in this introduction are two additional resources that might be helpful to presenters of this session. The first is the definition of "mathematical proficiency" from the book *Adding It Up: Helping Children Learn Mathematics* (Figure 1, p. 6) written by the National Research Council. Mathematical proficiency is visualized as five strands of mathematics—conceptual understanding, procedural fluency, strategic competence, adaptive reasoning, and productive disposition—that are interdependent and interwoven to form a sturdy, tightly connected representation of mathematical proficiency. As a visual, it may be useful in helping parents understand *all* the different aspects involved in creating mathematically powerful students.

The second is the chart "What Can Parents Do?" developed by MEC's Public Session Development Team (p. 7). It outlines the roles parents can assume in their child's mathematical education. Though the chart had originally been intended to use with parents, it seemed cumbersome; however, it may help a presenter think about the goals and focus of a particular session, or it may be adapted to use with parents in shorter sessions over a longer period of time or series of workshops. With this in mind, it also is included in the handout section of each session.

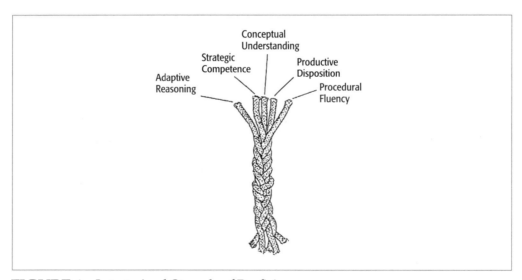

FIGURE 1: *Intertwined Strands of Proficiency*

	... as an Adult?	... as a Parent?	... with Your Child at Home?	... for Your Child at School?
Parent as a Learner	• continue to learn and be a learner of mathematics • recognize that mathematics is an important tool for making sense of the world around you • recognize that new discoveries are still being made in mathematics	• learn what math is all about for your child • pay attention to experiences that impact your child's attitudes about mathematics	• investigate and play with numbers • involve your child in the measuring and comparing that you do at home • use games to support mathematical thinking • do mental arithmetic and share strategies	• attend parent math nights • look for information that comes home about your school's mathematics program • become familiar with mathematics as it is taught in your child's classroom
Parent as a Researcher	• be curious about how you and others solve problems • broaden your understanding of what mathematics is • find out about current research in mathematics teaching and learning	• ask questions to understand your child's thinking • be curious about how your child solves problems	• investigate with your child his or her mathematical questions • explore with your child the best time and place to do homework	• ask questions about your child's mathematics program, both the goals and how it is taught • find out about roles for parents in the mathematics program at your child's school
Parent as a Communicator	• recognize that learning and understanding mathematics depends on communication (listening, talking, and writing) • learn to examine and explain your own thinking	• share information with your child about how you use mathematics • display a positive disposition about mathematics	• talk with your child about the importance of mathematics in his or her life • explore the many ways to approach solving problems • be clear about your expectations for homework • find ways to show enthusiasm about mathematics	• find a way to let the school know what you want for your child's mathematical education • become a knowledgeable advocate for good mathematics education

Presenter's Guide

Sample Workshop Agenda

7:00   Welcome and Introduction

7:10   Multiplication Facts and Concepts

7:50   Working Toward Fluency

8:40   What About Drill and Practice?

8:50   Closing

Sample Workshop Agenda with Activity Detail

7:00   Introduction to Workshop
Welcome
Overview of Goals for Workshop

7:10   Multiplication Facts and Concepts
Circles and Stars
Multiplication Rectangles
Building a Multiplication Table
Designs Found in Multiples

7:50   Working Toward Fluency
Patterns in the Multiplication Table

8:40   What About Drill and Practice?
Multiplication Tic-Tac-Toe
Brian Bangel

8:50   Closing
Collect Response Forms
Thanks and Good Night
Q & A

Materials Needed

For Presenter

overhead projector

prepared overhead transparencies

blank overhead transparencies

overhead transparency pens

cutouts of transparent paper rectangles sized (1×1), (1×2), (1×3), (1×4), (2×2), (1×5), (1×6), (2×3), (1×7), (1×8), (2×4), (1×10), (2×5), (1×9), (3×3), (1×12), (2×6), (3×4), (1×16), (2×8), (4×4) to match grid in Overhead 4

underlying blank grid in Overhead 4

one die

four color tiles for overhead

ten copies of Overhead 5 colored with multiple patterns for 2, 3, 4, 5, 6, 7, 8, 9, 10, and 12.

Overhead 7 with multiples of 3 circled

two paperclips

optional: multiplication wall of student work (see p. 52)

optional: colored game chips

wet paper towels

For Participants

duplicates of handouts—one copy per person

optional: two paperclips per group of four participants

optional: colored game chips

Room arrangement should enable participants to work in pairs.

Overview and Goals

Notes for Presenter

This session has been developed for a group of parents who may or may not have attended another parent session. That is, relative to both its goals and mathematics content, this workshop is designed to stand alone.

The workshop directions are meant to guide your planning and facilitate your preparation, not dictate your words or actions. You need to make decisions about whether the structure and content make sense for your situation. The constraints of the room, time, numbers of parents, and personal style may necessitate some adjustments to various details.

Goals for the Session

Participants will:

◆ learn what it means to teach multiplication for understanding

◆ experience drill and practice in an engaging problem-solving context

◆ understand the distinction between knowing multiplication facts and simply memorizing them

Other ideas we hope parents encounter during this particular session:

◆ Mathematics is engaging and motivating.

◆ When children learn multiplication with deep understanding, they see how it relates to many other mathematical ideas.

Detailed Directions for a 2-Hour Session

Preparation

Prior to the session, organize all of the transparent cutout rectangles for 1, 2, 3, 4, 5, 6, 7, 8, 9, 12, and 16 on an overhead transparency in preparation for the "Multiplication Rectangles" section of the session found on page 21.

Welcome, Introduction, and Goals (10 MINUTES)

Opening the Session

Introduce yourself and welcome the participants.

SAY *Good evening. Thank you for taking the time to come this evening. I hope that you will find it a very worthwhile use of your time. This session was designed to address a question that we have been asked and that we have seen misrepresented in newspaper and Internet articles. The question is, "Why don't teachers care about children knowing their basic facts anymore?"*

In fact, we do care. It is not possible to be mathematically powerful without facility with numbers. Arithmetic is very important to the doing of mathematics.

The question we should be asking is not "Do children need to know their 'basic facts'?" but rather "What does it mean to 'know basic facts,' and how can we help children learn their facts while still teaching important mathematics?"

Contrary to what you may have heard or read, mathematics educators care a great deal about this issue. Some wonderful and innovative mathematics resources have been developed for this very purpose.

This is an interactive session. I am hoping you will feel comfortable sharing your thinking. I won't call on you unless you volunteer.

OVERHEAD 1

Workshop Goals

Participants will:

- understand what it means to teach multiplication for understanding

- experience drill and practice in an engaging problem-solving context

- understand the distinction between knowing multiplication facts and simply memorizing them

OVERHEAD 2

Workshop Agenda

- Welcome, Introduction, and Goals
- Multiplication Facts and Concepts
  - Circles and Stars
  - Multiplication Rectangles
  - Building a Multiplication Table
  - Designs Found in Multiples
- Working Toward Fluency: Patterns in the Multiplication Table
- What About Drill and Practice?
  - Multiplication Tic-Tac-Toe
  - Brian Frenkle
- Reflect on Goals

Introduce Goals

Display Overhead 1 and review the goals for the session.

SAY *This evening we will take a look at several weeks' worth of lessons designed to ensure that children understand multiplication and become fluent with the multiplication tables.*

To help us meet these goals, here is our agenda for tonight.

Display and review Overhead 2.

SAY *In a previous parent session, you may have heard talk about how norm-referenced standardized testing practices have tended to push more and more abstract ideas down earlier into the grades. Multiplication tends to be a classic example of this practice.*

I don't know if you remember learning your multiplication tables, but most of us were taught them in the fourth grade. Today, some people believe that we raise standards if we expect children to know their multiplication facts by second grade. We should consider seriously whether this raises standards or if the practice simply comes at the expense of a solid understanding of number relationships that children will need in order to be successful with mathematics.

If I could talk with every third-grade teacher, which I can't, I would suggest that third grade is the appropriate time to begin to give children lots of what we call "multiplicative experiences"—experiences that help them understand multiplication.

I generally refer people to two resources—first, if your school is using the K–5 program **Investigations In Number, Data and Space,** *then the teacher should teach the multiplication sessions as designed because they are focused units that develop understanding. If, however, your school does not have this resource or another that contains a focused approach to multiplication, then I would suggest that the teacher use a book called* **Teaching Arithmetic: Lessons for Introducing Multiplication, Grade 3** *by Marilyn Burns. This is a multiweek unit written for third grade that has children experience multiplication in a variety of contexts. For example, one context is a game called Circles and Stars.*

A good resource to help children learn multiplication on a conceptual level is the book *Teaching Arithmetic: Lessons for Introducing Multiplication, Grade 3* by Marilyn Burns.

Multiplication Facts and Concepts (40 MINUTES)

Circles and Stars *(Burns 2001)* *(10 out of 40 minutes)*

Use a blank overhead to illustrate the game as follows. Draw a horizontal line in the middle of the overhead. Explain the game without bringing someone to the overhead to play with you.

You will need a blank transparency for Circles and Stars. The top half of the overhead represents your page (or playing space) and the bottom half represents your partner's page (or playing space).

SAY *This game is meant to be played with a partner. On my turn I roll the die. I rolled a 4, so that tells me to put four circles on my page.*

Model by placing four circles on the top half of the overhead.

SAY *Now it's my partner's turn. She rolled a 3, so she puts three circles on her page.*

Model again by placing three circles on the lower half of the overhead.

SAY *Now I rolled a 3. This roll of the die tells me to put three stars in each of my circles.*

Model by placing three stars in each circle in the upper half of the overhead.

SAY **(While modeling)** *Notice that children are learning that multiplication is about things that come in equal-size groups.*

If we care about the mathematical context that this problem is embedded in, then I will ask my students several questions.

Ask the audience the following questions, pausing a short time after each.

SAY *Is it possible for my partner to have more stars than I have after her next roll? What is the probability my partner will have more stars than I do after her next roll? What will it take for my partner to have more stars than I do after her next roll?*

Correct response is a roll of a five or a six.

SAY *So there are two things that could happen that will result in my partner having more stars than I have. How many different events are possible on her next roll?*

Correct response is six.

SAY *Are they all equally likely? Is she as likely to roll a 4 as a 1 or any other number?*

Correct responses are both "yes."

Write 2/6 on the overhead.

SAY *There are two out of six equally likely events that will result in her having more stars.*

Write Prob(more stars) = 2/6.

SAY *We would write that the probability of her having more stars than I have is 2/6 or 1/3.*

SAY *Children play lots of rounds of Circles and Stars and then they label each round. So in this case I would write "4 sets of 3 stars" or "4 × 3 = 12."*

Write 4 x 3 = 12 on the overhead under the four circles.

SAY *Normally, we would gather data from students in the classroom, as on this overhead. The products would be tallied and anyone who got a product of 12 would put a tally mark by 12, and so on.*

Display Overhead 3.

OVERHEAD 3

	Circles and Stars—Data Collection		
1	### /	19	
2	### ### /	20	### ### //
3	### ###	21	
4	### ### ### ////	22	
5	### ### /	23	
6	### ### ### ### /	24	### ### //
7		25	### /
8	### ###	26	
9	### /	27	
10	### ### /	28	
11		29	
12	### ### ### ### ###	30	### ////
13		31	
14		32	
15	### ###	33	
16	////	34	
17		35	
18	### ### ////	36	### ////

SAY *After we've collected the classroom data on a chart, we analyze the data. We want children collecting and analyzing data. When we look at the data we notice some interesting things. For example, one thing we notice is that there are no tally marks after the 7. Do you have any idea why this would be true?*

Possible response:

✔ Someone will likely say, "There's no 7 on the die."

SAY *There is no 10 either, but we have tally marks after the 10. So why do you think there would not be tally marks after the 7?*

At this point someone is likely to mention that 7 is a prime number. Review for the audience that 7 is a prime number, which means it has only two factors, 1 and 7. Because there is no 7 on the die, it is impossible to get a 7.

SAY *There are other interesting things we notice in the data. For example, 12 has a lot of tally marks. Do you have any idea why 12 would have more tallies than some of the other numbers?*

Expect this response:

✔ Someone may say something such as, "There are more ways to make 12."

SAY *Yes, 12 has more factors between 1 and 6 than some of the other numbers, so there are more ways to make 12 by rolling the two dice.*

Circles and Stars is just one of several different contexts for multiplication in the book **Teaching Arithmetic.** *Again, with third graders we want to provide lots of opportunities to multiply in contexts that build an understanding of multiplication.*

At the end of this unit, some third graders will still count to find out how many stars there are with four circles of three stars. It might not make us happy to see this, but developmentally, some third graders will be there. Some third graders will count, 3, 6, 9, 12, and some will just know that 4 times 3 is 12. We can expect this range. So multiplication is not finished in third grade, but it is the appropriate grade to begin to focus on multiplication.

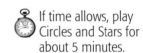 If time allows, play Circles and Stars for about 5 minutes.

💡 You might want to put the sample Circles and Stars game back on the overhead.

Multiplication Rectangle *(Burns 1993)* *(10 out of 40 minutes)*

SAY *If I could talk to all fourth-grade teachers, which I can't, I would say, "If your textbook does not provide a focused approach to multiplication, please consider using a sequence of lessons in the book* **A Collection of Math Lessons: Grades 3 through 6** *by Marilyn Burns."* *We'll take a quick look at the series of lessons on multiplication in this book.*

💡 Many new curricular materials introduce multiplication using a geometric model.

A good resource for activities that help children learn on a conceptual level is the book *A Collection of Math Lessons: Grades 3 through 6* by Marilyn Burns.

Put four color tiles on the overhead.

SAY *This unit starts by asking children to build all possible rectangles for the numbers 1 through 25. For example, what size solid rectangle can we make with these four squares?*

Expect that someone will say "1 by 4."

Make the rectangle that fits the number sentence the audience gives.

SAY *What else could we call this rectangle?*

Turn the rectangle as you repeat, "4 by 1."

SAY *Are there any other solid rectangles we could make with these squares?*

Expect that someone will say, "2 by 2."

You may want to prepare of sample of a classroom multiplication wall to use as a visual. See page 52 for information.

SAY *Now some of you are saying, "But that's a square." Many of us grew up believing that a square and a rectangle are two different things. A square is a special kind of rectangle. Are there any other rectangles we could build?*

What we just did with 4 squares, children are asked to do with all the numbers from 1 to 25, and they cut out all the possible rectangles. So they have a lot of data in front of them. I don't have all the data because it wouldn't fit on one sheet, but I have a lot of the data.

Put the transparency with all of the cutout rectangles on the overhead.

SAY *The first thing children do is label all the rectangles. For example* (pointing to the 3-by-2 rectangle), *how would they label this rectangle?*

Expect this response:

✔ If they say "2 by 3," ask how else this could be labeled ("3 by 2").

Label the 3-by-2 rectangle both ways.

SAY *Children will have a lot more data than this in front of them. When we ask them to analyze the data, again we notice some interesting things. For example, we notice that for some of these numbers we only have one rectangle. For example, 1 has only one rectangle, 2 has only one, 3 has only one, 5 has only one, 7 has only one. What do you think will be the next number to have only one rectangle?*

Expect the response of 11.

SAY *Why do you think it will be 11?*

Expect the answer:

✔ It is a prime number.

SAY *Yes, 11 is a prime number, so the only rectangle will be 11 by 1. Are all of those numbers I just mentioned prime numbers—1, 2, 3, 5, 7, 11? Contrary to what many of us learned, 1 is **not** a prime number. Do you know why?*

Reinforce the fact that a prime number must have exactly two *different* factors, one and itself. The number 1 only has one factor, so it is not prime.

SAY *When we look at the data we notice other interesting things. For example, with some of these numbers we can build squares. One has a square, 4 has a square, 9 has one, 16 has one. What number will have the next square?*

Expected response is 25.

SAY *Why do you think that? What do you know about those numbers 1, 4, 9, 16, 25?*

Expect that someone will say, "You can make squares."

SAY *Yes, they make squares and we call them square numbers. Some of us didn't really understand until we were adults that a square number is simply a number you can make a square from. We don't have to withhold this information from children!*

Children interpret the data in many more ways that help them as they begin to learn their multiplication facts.

Building a Multiplication Table *(10 out of 40 minutes)*

SAY *Once they have analyzed their rectangle data, they do another interesting thing with the data (all of their rectangles).*

Display Overhead 4.

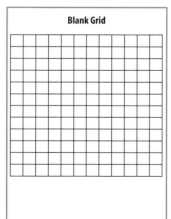

Overhead 4

Blank Grid

SAY *They take a blank grid like this and put a dot in the upper left-hand corner.*

Model by doing this on Overhead 4.

SAY *Then they take each rectangle, place it into the upper left-hand corner where the dot is, lift the bottom right-hand corner of the rectangle and write the number of squares in the small square on the grid.*

Demonstrate with the transparent cutout 4-by-2 rectangle, writing an 8 in the square on the grid that matches the bottom right-hand corner of the cutout rectangle.

Next, rotate the rectangle in the other direction, again place it into the upper left-hand corner, lift the bottom right-hand corner and write the 8 again on the corresponding square on the grid.

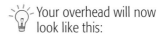
Your overhead will now look like this:

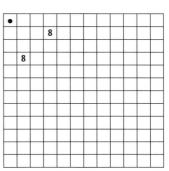

SAY *Now, some of you are going to make a discovery during the next few moments. Please do not turn to someone and tell him or her what you see. If you make a discovery, please be careful not to reveal it to anyone else. Telling someone an answer is rarely helpful, because it robs that person of the opportunity to make their own discovery. So, please do not tell.*

Continue the process above with several other rectangles. After a few moments, stop and ask the audience what they notice.

SAY *What is happening here?*

Expect this response:

✔ "You're building a multiplication table."

SAY *Yes, we're building a multiplication table. Do you remember those yellow folders we used to have in school that were called Pee-Chees? They used to have a small multiplication table on the back. Some of us were excited that we could find the answer to multiplication problems on the Pee-Chee, but we had no idea why the numbers were where they were. Instead, with this lesson, children are using the rectangles to build the multiplication table so that they do know why the numbers are there.*

Once students use their rectangles to complete the multiplication table, they do another interesting thing with the tables.

Designs Found in Multiples *(10 out of 40 minutes)*

See the Math Notes section on page 52. Make ten copies of Overhead 5. Color each one to replicate the plaid, and design patterns of the multiples of 2, 3, 4, 5, 6, 7, 8, 9, 10, 12 (but not 11) (see pp. 55–57).

You will want to label each overhead with the factor number on top so it will be easier to find the correct overhead mutiple pattern as you show different multiples again and again while testing participants' conjectures.

Place the multiples of 6 pattern on the overhead with the pattern covered up showing only the multiples of 6 you have written down the right-hand side of the chart.

SAY *This student had to first write all the multiples of 6 down the right-hand side until she reached 144.*

Uncover the first row and then the second row as you continue talking.

SAY *Wherever she saw a multiple of 6, she colored it in. For example, here is a 6, a 12, and an 18. When she colors in all the multiples of 6, an interesting pattern emerges.*

Uncover the Multiples of 6 Overhead.

SAY *Other children are doing the same for other numbers.*
This child did multiples of 2.

Display an overhead showing the patterns for the
multiples of 2.

SAY *This child did multiples of 3.*

Display the pattern for 3.

You may want to remind
participants that children
first write all the multiples to
144 down the right-hand side
of the design. Then they color
in the multiples and begin to
look for patterns.

SAY *Now we start to notice something—some of these pat-*
terns are just plaids, or straight lines like 3. But, some of
the patterns, like 4, have designs inside the plaids.

Display the multiples of 4 pattern.

SAY *What do you think will happen with the Multiples of 5?*
Will it have only plaids? Or will it have designs within
the plaids?

Listen to predictions, then show the 5s pattern on the
overhead.

SAY *Multiples of 6 had designs* (**as you put the 6 pattern**
back on the overhead). *What do you think will hap-*
pen with 7?

Once people have made some guesses, show the
pattern for 7.

SAY *What about 8?*

Pause for responses, then show the 8 pattern.

SAY *What about 9?*

Expect this response:

✔ Some people will say "straight lines or plaids" and some will say "designs."

SAY *Those of you who think it will be plaids or straight lines, what is your reasoning?*

Expect someone to say, "odd or even."

SAY *What about those of you who think it will be designs? What are you basing this on?*

Expect this response:

✔ Someone will say something like, "more factors."

~Be sure to wait until you hear both responses. This allows the group to test different conjectures.

~Primes have no design in the middle (just rows and columns).

SAY *What do we call those numbers that have more than two factors?*

Be sure to introduce the term *composites*.

SAY *Well, here is the pattern for 9.*

Put the 9s pattern on the overhead.

SAY *So, can it be odd and even?*

Expect a "No" response.

SAY *Could it still be primes and composites?*

Expect a "Yes" response.

SAY *So what do you think will happen with 10s?*

Get a response from the audience before proceeding.

SAY *What about 11?*

Let the audience respond.

SAY *Are you sure? I wish I had an 11. "Let me know what you find out," is what I would say to my students.*

What about 12?

After taking participant responses, show the 12s pattern.

SAY *Now this is not really fair. With children, these patterns are posted around the room. Tonight, I'm putting them up on the overhead and taking them away so it is difficult for you to see the patterns.*

Once the patterns are all posted, we have children analyze the patterns and we notice interesting things once again. For example, does the 12s pattern have a line of symmetry?

Give time for the audience to figure this out.

The 12s pattern should still be on the overhead. At this point, you may decide to display one chart paper with small copies of the multiples (2–12).

SAY *Children will do just what you are doing* (turn your head as if you are trying to figure it out), *so there are spatial relationships involved here as well.*

Show me with your arm where the line of symmetry is . . . if you think there is one.

Test the line by folding the overhead pattern along the diagonal line of symmetry so participants can see the visual match.

SAY *But what about the 5s design?*

Put the 5s design back on the overhead.

SAY *Does it have a line of symmetry? Again, show me with your arm where you think the line of symmetry might be.*

Expect this response:

✔ Some people will hold their arm horizontally.

SAY *Some of you are holding your arm horizontally like this* (model), *let's try that out.*

Fold the design in the middle and note that the two sides do not match up.

SAY *Some of you think it is the same diagonal as before.*

Fold along the diagonal to test this and the design will match up.

SAY *What about the design for 8?*

Put the 8s design on the overhead.

SAY *Does it have a line of symmetry?*

Have the audience predict and then test it.

SAY *What we begin to notice is that every one of these designs has that same line of symmetry. Why do you think that is true?*

Wait a moment to give reflection time and perhaps a chance to respond.

SAY *Students think it is because multiplication is commutative, because "3 times 4" is equal to "4 times 3." Students know this because they make a connection. They remember building the multiplication table by placing the rectangles in each direction so they know we built the table around that line of symmetry.*

Working Toward Fluency (50 MINUTES)

Patterns in the Multiplication Table

SAY *If children have had rich experiences that foster a conceptual understanding of multiplication in third grade and the beginning of the fourth grade, some children will end fourth grade knowing all of their multiplication facts and some will end knowing some but not all of the multiplication facts.*

What we are going to do next is generally appropriate for late fourth grade on up through high school. If middle or high school students are not yet fluent with their multiplication facts, then I think teachers should take about a week to have students do the sequence of experiences we are about to do. Again, this is a sequence that is very appropriate for children at the end of fourth grade and on up.

Multiplication Chart

×	1	2	3	4	5	6	7	8	9	10
1	1	2	3	4	5	6	7	8	9	10
2	2	4	6	8	10	12	14	16	18	20
3	3	6	9	12	15	18	21	24	27	30
4	4	8	12	16	20	24	28	32	36	40
5	5	10	15	20	25	30	35	40	45	50
6	6	12	18	24	30	36	42	48	54	60
7	7	14	21	28	35	42	49	56	63	70
8	8	16	24	32	40	48	56	64	72	80
9	9	18	27	36	45	54	63	72	81	90
10	10	20	30	40	50	60	70	80	90	100

Put Overhead 5, the 10-by-10 multiplication chart, on the overhead.

SAY *Students staple this on the inside cover of their mathematics learning log. I tell them that we're going to work on our multiplication facts until they know them with ease, but that I don't expect them to be hard to learn as they already know quite a few. I ask them if there are any facts they already know.*

Is there anything you already know?

Expect someone will say 1s.

SAY *You know your ones?*

Cover the sheet before continuing.

SAY *Six times 1? One times 8? You know your 1s, so let's get rid of those.*

Color in the 1s row and 1s column.

SAY *Is there anything else you already know?*

Expect someone will say 10s.

Cover the table and ask a couple of 10s questions, then color in the 10s row and 10s column.

SAY *Is there anything else you already know?*

Expect that someone will say 2s or 5s.

SAY *Almost all fifth graders come knowing their 2s. There are exceptions, but the exceptions are rare. Let me see if you know your 2s.*

Cover up the table and ask some 'times 2' questions. Color in the 2s column and 2s row on the multiplication table. Continue doing the same for the 5s.

SAY *The other thing most children (especially those who have done the rectangle lessons we saw before) say they know is the "square numbers." Let me see if you know your square numbers.*

Cover the table and ask some square number questions. Color in the square numbers on the diagonal.

SAY *After having crossed out just what they know— the 1s, 2s, 5s, and 10s and square numbers—there are now just 15 facts left to learn.*

Count them as you say this.

Be sure to place Overhead 5 in a spot so you can easily find it again.

SAY *That is, if you understand that multiplication is commutative. If you know that 3 times 4 is the same as 4 times 3, then all of this . . . (cover right side of diagonal with your hand) is the same as this.*

Cover left of diagonal with your hand. Record the number 15 on the transparency to the right of the table you are coloring in.

SAY *Now we would ask children what they want to learn next. Typically children will say 9s because some of them have learned tricks for 9s.*

SAY *Although tricks are fine, we don't really need them. What we would do with children is put just the 9s tables on a chart on the wall and ask children to record any patterns they can find. I'd like for you to work with someone near you and look for interesting patterns in the 9s table. Be ready to share the patterns you find.*

Uncover the multiples of 9 table by erasing those colored squares in the vertical 9s column. Some of the 9s will have been colored in during earlier questions. The entire column of 9s must be clear for this next question. Give the audience about two minutes to look for patterns in the 9s table, then call the group back together.

SAY *Did anyone find a pattern you would be willing to share?*

Expect this response:

✔ The two typical patterns that come up first are generally the following:

(1) The 1s digits decrease by one and the 10s digits increase by one. When this pattern comes up:

SAY *I would like to focus on just the 10s digit. If I want the product of 9 times 7, is there a way to know what the 10s digit will be without having to count?*

Expect this response:

✔ Expect that someone will say that it will be one less than the number you are multiplying 9 by.

SAY *So if I want to do 9 times 7, I know the 10s digit will be what? 6. So it will be sixty-something. What if I want to do 9 times 4? (The 10s digit will be 3.) So it will be thirty-something.*

(2) The digits always add to 9. When this pattern comes up, check it on the table.

SAY *I want to see if these two patterns will help us learn our 9s tables. For 9 times 5, what will the 10s digit be? 4. So that's 40. Forty-what? 45. Is 4 plus 5 equal to 9? What about 9 times 8? 9 times 3?*

So, just by using patterns the 9s table becomes very simple. It usually only takes a few minutes for children to say they know their 9s facts so we can move on. Since I want them to know that mathematics is about a search for patterns, I continue to ask, "Who saw another pattern?"

Ask the audience for other patterns. If no one mentions it, note that the digits reverse when you get to 54, and that "9 times 2" is the same as "10 times 2 minus 2," and so on.

SAY *Again, with children it usually takes a very short time for them to be comfortable with their 9s.*

Display Overhead 6 again. This time cross the 9s column and the 9s row off the multiplication table.

SAY *Having just crossed out what they already knew, then working on the 9s facts for about 15 to 20 minutes, we now have just ten facts left to learn.*

Record 10 under the 15 to the right of the table on the transparency.

Place Overhead 6 in a place so you can easily find it again.

SAY *Once they've gotten past their tricks, children typically like to make life easy so they usually ask to learn their 3s next. We would put just the 3s facts on a chart and ask students to record any patterns they can find. Again, work with someone next to you to find any patterns you can in the 3s table.*

Display the multiples of 3 table this time by erasing those colored squares in the vertical 3s column as done earlier for the 9s.

Give the audience a minute to work, then call them back together. Ask them if anyone is willing to share a pattern they noticed.

Expect the following patterns to arise. If they don't, share them as patterns that children notice:

✔ The digits add to multiples of 3.

✔ The pattern is odd, even, and so on.

✔ In the 10s digit, there are three 0s, then three 1s, then three 2s.

If time allows, you might want to explore why.

SAY *Do you think that if we extended the table this last pattern would continue? Test it out. Can you predict how the pattern will continue?*

Another way to look for patterns in multiples is to use a 0 to 99 chart. I would begin a pattern by circling a few numbers (for example, 0, 3, 6, 9, and 12). I would only circle a few, because we want children doing the work. Once they have circled all the multiples of 3, I again ask them to record any patterns they can find.

Display Overhead 6 with multiples of 3 circled.

OVERHEAD 6

Zero to Ninety-Nine Chart									
0	1	2	3	4	5	6	7	8	9
10	11	12	13	14	15	16	17	18	19
20	21	22	23	24	25	26	27	28	29
30	31	32	33	34	35	36	37	38	39
40	41	42	43	44	45	46	47	48	49
50	51	52	53	54	55	56	57	58	59
60	61	62	63	64	65	66	67	68	69
70	71	72	73	74	75	76	77	78	79
80	81	82	83	84	85	86	87	88	89
90	91	92	93	94	95	96	97	98	99

SAY *I would like for you to work with someone near you and look for patterns in the multiples of 3. Please continue until you have found at least six interesting patterns.*

Give the group two or three minutes to explore patterns, then call them back together.

Participants may use the 0 to 99 chart in their handouts.

SAY *Is anyone willing to share an interesting pattern you found?*

The following patterns often arise. If they don't, share these as patterns children typically find.

✔ In the circled diagonals that run right to left, the digits add up to consecutive multiples of 3.

SAY *What if we extended the table? Would this be true? Sure enough, we get 3, 6, 9, 12, 15, 18, 21, 24, 27, 30, 33, and so on—all the multiples of 3.*

✔ With the circled numbers on the diagonals that run left to right, the digits add up to a consecutive multiple of 3. Again, emphasize multiples of 3, 6, 9, and so on.

✔ With the circled numbers on any column, the digits add to consecutive multiples of 3.

SAY *And again we see 3, 6, 9. 12, 15, 18, and so on.*

Instead of using timed tests or flash cards or practice with isolated facts that we hope stay in children's minds . . . and we know they stick for some children and not for others . . . we can instead teach in a more brain-compatible way, by using just the 3s table and searching for patterns. What comes up over and over is the pattern of multiples, 3, 6, 9, 12, 15, 18, 21, 24, 27, 30, 33, and so on. We don't need to teach multiplication facts in ways that result in many children learning to fear and avoid math.

Who sees another pattern?

Expected response:

✔ If you look at the diagonal that runs from 0 in the upper left-hand corner to the 99 in the lower right, in the diagonals of circled numbers around that diagonal, the digits are reversed, for example, 15, 51, and so on.

Understanding Multiplication Across the Grades

SAY *See if you can follow this pattern that a fifth grader suggested: "If you take any circle up there, add the next two numbers, then subtract the circle, you will get the next circle."*

💡 You may want to tell the audience that you didn't follow it the first time you heard it either. Repeat the pattern and example.

Did you follow that? Take the circled 3. Adding the next two numbers, 4 + 5 = 9. And, 9 − 3 = 6, or the next circled number after 3.

Will this always work? When I ask children this question, I provide a context for drill, but drill that is engaging because we are trying to test whether or not a pattern will always work.

What I'm going to do next is generally appropriate for fifth graders on up. There are exceptions. A few children are ready for challenges earlier than is typical, but generally this next step makes sense for fifth grade on up.

*Let's see if we can determine whether that pattern will always work. What if I call any circle here (n) with (n) being a variable. It can be this circle (**pointing to circles**), this circle, or any circle here. That is basically what a variable is. If I call this circle (n), then we're going to add two numbers together to test this pattern. What will the first number be?*

💡 Write on the bottom part of the 0 to 99 chart.

Write the expression ($n + 1$) on the overhead as the audience suggests it.

SAY *What will the second number be?*

Write ($n + 2$).

SAY *What do we get if we add (n + 1) and (n + 2)?*

Write $2n + 3$.

SAY *To check this pattern, we need to subtract something. What will it be?*

Expect that someone will say, "the circle."

SAY *What did we call the circle?*

Write (*n*).

SAY *What is 2n + 3 – (n)?*

Your recording may look like this:

$$\textcircled{n}\ (n + 1) + (n + 2) = 2n + 3$$
$$\underline{\qquad\qquad\qquad - n}$$
$$n + 3$$

Record *n* + 3.

SAY *Will that always be the next multiple of 3? Sure, that's how we get multiples of three, by adding three to the previous multiple.*

Here is another pattern that a fifth grader found. Try to follow this one. If you take any two consecutive multiples of 3 circles and add them, you will get the same sum as you would get when you add the two numbers between them. Did you follow that pattern?

Test the student's pattern with two consecutive circles (multiples of 3).

SAY *But will this always work? Again, when I ask this question, I have provided an opportunity for drill and practice with addition.*

SAY *Again, let's see if we can determine whether this pattern will always work. If I call the first of any two consecutive circles (n), with (n) being a variable, then we are going to add something to (n). What will we be adding?*

Record $(n) + (n + 3)$.

Again, record on the bottom of the 0 to 99 chart.

SAY *What do we get when we add (n) plus (n + 3)?*

Record $(2n + 3)$.

SAY *If we're going to check this pattern we'll be adding two other numbers together. What will the first number be?*

Record $(n + 1)$.

SAY *What will we add to (n + 1)?*

Record $(n + 2)$.

SAY *What do we get when we add (n + 1) and (n + 2)?*

Record $(2n + 3)$.

SAY *Will we always get the same number?*

Circle the two $(2n + 3)$s.

At this point, your written recording may look like this:

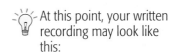

$$n + (n + 3) = \boxed{2n + 3}$$
and
$$(n + 1) + (n + 2) = \boxed{2n + 3}$$

SAY *These explorations can take some time. But in addition to focusing on the 3-times tables, what other mathematics are children doing?*

Some things that may be suggested are:

✔ searching for patterns

✔ looking at our number system

✔ using algebraic reasoning

✔ communicating their thinking

SAY *So, a lot of mathematics is involved.*

Display Overhead 6 again. Color in the 3s column and 3s row.

SAY *Let's get rid of the 3s. Now all we have done is the facts they already knew; the 9s took us only a few minutes and the 3s took us two or three days.*

Count the remaining facts left to learn (there should be 6) and record the 6 under the 10 on the overhead.

⏱ Before you continue, if time allows, you may want to include the Triangular Number discovery (see Math Notes, pages 58–60, for the script).

SAY *We have only six facts left to learn.*

Children are going to want to learn their 4s next, and you'll notice that there are not very many 4s left to learn.

And in the same way, we can use a 0 to 99 chart and circle multiples of 4 and see different patterns emerge—patterns that help us learn our 4s so that there are now only three more facts to learn.

So with the multiplication facts, either we can give children timed tests and flash cards and isolated drill or we can use the multiplication table to investigate patterns in multiples and explore our number system. Which approach do you think is more likely to result in students who understand multiplication, who want to do mathematics, and who enjoy it?

What About Drill and Practice? (10 MINUTES)

SAY We're often asked the question, "What about drill and practice? Is it important?" Yes, it is important. Whatever it is that we're trying to learn to do, doing lots of it often helps us to be able to do it with ease. But with math, it is very important that we understand what drill will and will not do.

Drill will not teach a mathematical concept. Now that is a bit hard to understand, but again, all the drill in the world will not teach a mathematical idea. Many of us taught for years thinking that it would. We often taught believing that if we just gave children one more page of problems they would get it.

We now understand that this is not where "getting it" comes from. But once we have given children opportunities to understand multiplication and how it is used, then drill and practice can help them learn to use multiplication facts or relationships with ease.

Drill and practice with mathematics should be engaging and motivating and provided in contexts that ask children to think and reason and behave in mathematically important ways. It should result in kids who want to do mathematics.

Purpose: Participants will engage in a game that is motivating and provides practice with the multiplication facts.

One half of the room becomes the Xs (or red chips) and the other half of the room become the Os (or the blue chips).

OVERHEAD 7

Tic-Tac-Toe Products

1	2	3	4	5	6
7	8	9	10	12	14
15	16	18	20	21	24
25	27	28	30	32	35
36	40	42	45	48	49
54	56	63	64	72	81

0 1 2 3 4 5 6 7 8 9

SAY *One of my favorite games that provides drill with multiplication is in your packet. You won't need it right now, but we will play it for a few minutes so that you will know how to play it at home.*

Display Overhead 7.

Divide the audience into two teams (Xs and Os) and play Multiplication Tic-Tac-Toe, recording at the overhead.

SAY *Each team is trying to capture four numbers in a row horizontally, vertically, or diagonally. The way you capture a number is to tell me what factors you want the paper clips placed on. For example, if you said, "4 and 6," I would ask you what 4 times 6 is. If you told me 24, I would put your X or red chip on 24. After the opening move, each team can move only one paper clip. You can move it anywhere you would like, but you can only move one paper clip. It is OK to have both paper clips on the same number, such as $6 \times 6 = 36$. Let's play for a few minutes and the directions will be clear.*

Xs (or Reds), you won the toss. Where do you want to start? I need two factors.

Play the game with the whole group until each group has had at least four turns so that players get to think about strategies.

Place the paper clips on the two factors suggested and ask for the product. Remind the Os (or Blue Team) that they can now move only one paper clip. Continue the game until people have had a chance to think about strategies (about five minutes), then cover up the overhead.

SAY *Are you doing drill? Yes, you're considering several multiplication facts for each move you make. But for obvious reasons, this is not a good way for students to play the game.*

Some of you are trying to follow a strategy and I'm taking whoever is loudest, so you might be frustrated. Also, I know that some of you are doing drill and practice. But I don't know that all of you are.

It's not OK for one-sixth of the class to be tuned out. So, in the classroom we would have children seated in groups of four, give each group a game board, and have two children play two children.

The reason for having children work in partners is twofold. First, some children don't know their multiplication facts and it helps to talk them over as part of learning them. Second, some children don't see the strategies.

I hope we played the game long enough for you to see that this game is very sophisticated with regard to strategies—especially when you realize you not only need to pay attention to where you want to be but also to where you don't want to leave your opponents and where you might want to be positioned for your next move.

If time allows, have the participants play the game for a short time.

Once children catch on, the game takes a long time to play. It sometimes takes 45 minutes or more, and the wonderful thing is that children are practicing their multiplication facts for 45 minutes and no one is complaining.

We also send games like this home for homework, but we send it with a letter that says something such as

> *Dear Parents,*
>
> *We are working on learning multiplication facts this year. We will be doing a lot of practice. Please notice the practice you are doing while playing this game, and enjoy playing!*

We've learned that the letters are important because even though games like this go home for homework, parents often ask why they are not seeing drill coming home. We now realize that if parents are used to seeing drill look like 40 problems on a page, they won't necessarily notice that children might be doing 400-plus such problems in the context of playing a game that also asks them to think, reason, and behave in mathematically important ways.

We have to get a lot better at understanding that drill is very solidly embedded in the new programs we have available to us today. It just looks very different from what we were used to seeing.

If you think for a moment, though, about which approach is more likely to result in a child who learns to like mathematics, the reasonable choice seems pretty obvious.

Brian Bangel *(2 out of 10 minutes)*

SAY *I want to share one more story before we wrap things up this evening. This is a story of a third-grade boy named Brian Bangel. His teacher, Eva Byber, wrote about an experience with Brian.*

When Brian's class entered third grade not fluent with their addition facts, Ms. Byber decided to spend some time helping them become fluent. She started by giving children an addition table and asking them to find patterns in the table. After a few days of examining lots of different patterns, she began to use strategies for addition.

For example, she had children look at just the doubles until they knew 4 plus 4, 6 plus 6, 9 plus 9, and so on. Once children knew their doubles, she had them focus on doubles plus and minus one. Because children already knew 7 plus 7, then 6 plus 7 and 8 plus 7 were easy to figure out.

Once they knew their doubles plus and minus one, she taught them a method she called the "sharing method." The sharing method works for numbers that have a difference of two, for example, 7 plus 9.

She had children build a tower of seven blocks and a tower of nine blocks, take one block off of the 9 and put it on the 7, and notice that it was the same as twice the number in the middle. Because they already knew their doubles, they now knew problems like 6 plus 8, 5 plus 7, 4 plus 6, and so on.

You may want to have two block towers of interlocking cubes to demonstrate that $7 + 9 = 8 + 8$.

Ms. Byber wrote about Brian late in the year when the class had begun working on multiplication. She began the unit by giving children a multiplication table and asking them to look for patterns in the table.

Display Overhead 8 (a clean multiplication table).

OVERHEAD **8**

Multiplication Table

1	2	3	4	5	6	7	8	9	10	11	12
2	4	6	8	10	12	14	16	18	20	22	24
3	6	9	12	15	18	21	24	27	30	33	36
4	8	12	16	20	24	28	32	36	40	44	48
5	10	15	20	25	30	35	40	45	50	55	60
6	12	18	24	30	36	42	48	54	60	66	72
7	14	21	28	35	42	49	56	63	70	77	84
8	16	24	32	40	48	56	64	72	80	88	96
9	18	27	36	45	54	63	72	81	90	99	108
10	20	30	40	50	60	70	80	90	100	110	120
11	22	33	44	55	66	77	88	99	110	121	132
12	24	36	48	60	72	84	96	108	120	132	144

SAY *About three days into this search for patterns, Brian walked into class and told Ms. Byber that he had found a sharing method for multiplication. This surprised Ms. Byber because she hadn't known there was one.*

When she asked Brian to explain what he had found, he said it works with numbers that are two apart, just like the sharing method for addition. Brian said that if you want to multiply two numbers, say 7 and 9, you would take the number between them, which is what? (8) Multiply that number by itself, which would be what? (64) Then subtract 1, which is what? (63). Isn't that 7 times 9?

Ms. Byber told Brian that this was very interesting and asked him if it always works. Brian responded, "Try it."

Do you think it will always work? What about with double-digit numbers? For example, what about 19 times 21? Could you multiply 20 times 20? What would you get? (400) Minus 1, what do you have? (399) Is that 19 times 21? Well, we don't know easily, but we now have a context for caring about double-digit multiplication because we want to know if Brian's pattern will always work.

I am going to let you investigate Brian's pattern on your own and try to discover if and why it always works. It is a wonderful investigation.

What struck me most about Brian's story is that he was not in a classroom where the teacher thought, "OK, Brian, that's neat, but you're supposed to be memorizing your multiplication facts so let's get busy."

He was also not in a classroom where the teacher believed something that we hear a lot in this national debate about education, that is, "OK, problem solving is important but it doesn't belong in the curriculum before children have learned their basic facts."

If Brian had been in this kind of classroom, I do not think he would have invented the sharing method for multiplication. None of his classmates would know it. I wouldn't know it. I didn't know there was a sharing method until I heard Brian's story. I doubt many of you would have known it.

Brian had the great fortune of being in a classroom with a teacher who understood that everything we teach— yes, everything we teach, including basic facts—should be taught consistent with the message that mathematics is a sense-making process. And everything we teach, including basic facts, needs to be taught in a manner consistent with the message that mathematics is about a search for patterns and relationships in the world around us.

Ms. Byber began the unit by having children look for patterns in the multiplication table. Brian discovered that when you look at this diagonal (point to diagonal from the upper left-hand corner to the lower right on Overhead 8) . . .

We see a 9 and an 8 and 8; a 16 and a 15 and 15, a 25 and a 24 and 24, and so on. When Brian discovered this pattern he didn't think it was there for no reason, because they had spent time earlier in the year exploring patterns in addition and discovering why the patterns work. So when he discovered this pattern he wanted to know why it works.

Closing (10 MINUTES)

SAY *We're often asked if it really matters how we teach multiplication facts as long as we teach them. We believe it absolutely matters.*

Put Overhead 9 on the overhead and go over each point.

> One approach results in children who may or may not know their multiplication tables.
>
> vs.
>
> The other teaches …

SAY (When you get to the last point) *After tonight's experiences, what would you say it teaches?*

List participants' responses on an overhead.

Expect responses such as:

✔ multiplication facts and patterns

✔ area of rectangles

✔ probability

✔ vocabulary of math

✔ algebraic reasoning

✔ generalization

✔ logic

✔ cummutativity

✔ data collection

✔ data analysis

✔ triangular numbers

✔ square numbers

✔ +, −, ÷

✔ number theory

✔ variables

Place a blank transparency on the overhead.

SAY *When we teach multiplication by timed tests and flash cards, what are children learning?*

List audience responses.

Expect responses such as:

✔ speed

✔ fear of math

✔ belief that I'm not very good

SAY *So, which approach is more likely to result in children who say "yes" to math?*

Thank you for taking the time out of your busy lives to come this evening to hear about mathematics education. I hope the session was helpful to you. Please take a minute to fill out the Participant Response Form. For those of you who have questions, I'm happy to stay and respond to them. If you have commitments and have to leave, please feel free to do so. Again, thank you for coming.

Answer participants' questions. Collect Participant Response Forms.

🔅 To prepare for participant questions, you will want to review the Q & A section of the companion booklet, *A Planning Handbook for Presenters.*

Multiplication Wall

In the Multiplication Rectangles activity (pages 21–31), children are asked to cut out all the rectangles (rectangular arrays) that they can make using squares from 1–25. Rectangles are labeled (for example, 2×3, 3×2). Then all cutout rectangular arrays are mounted on colored paper as shown.

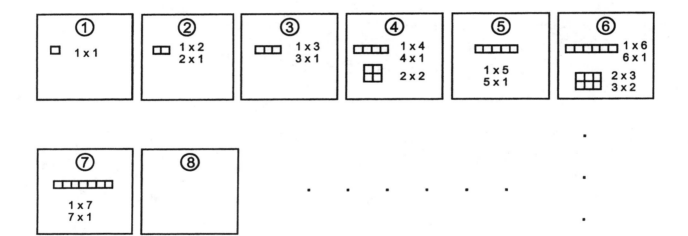

Math Notes (2)

Designs Found in Multiplication

Directions: Use Overhead 5 to make a separate, full-sized overhead for each of the multiples of 2, 3, 4, 5, 6, 7, 8, 9, 10, 12 (but not 11).

Use permanent marker (red) to color each overhead to replicate the plaid/design patterns on pages 55–57.

On the multiples of 6 design, write the multiples of 6 up to 144 down the right-hand side of the chart.

You may want to flag each overhead with the multiple number on a brightly colored sticky note so it will be easier to locate them as you display the different designs again and again while testing/confirming participants' conjectures.

1	2	3	4	5	6	7	8	9	10	11	12
2	4	6	8	10	12	14	16	18	20	22	24
3	6	9	12	15	18	21	24	27	30	33	36
4	8	12	16	20	24	28	32	36	40	44	48
5	10	15	20	25	30	35	40	45	50	55	60
6	12	18	24	30	36	42	48	54	60	66	72
7	14	21	28	35	42	49	56	63	70	77	84
8	16	24	32	40	48	56	64	72	80	88	96
9	18	27	36	45	54	63	72	81	90	99	108
10	20	30	40	50	60	70	80	90	100	110	120
11	22	33	44	55	66	77	88	99	110	121	132
12	24	36	48	60	72	84	96	108	120	132	144

Understanding Multiplication Across the Grades

Multiples of 2

1	2	3	4	5	6	7	8	9	10	11	12
2	4	6	8	10	12	14	16	18	20	22	24
3	6	9	12	15	18	21	24	27	30	33	36
4	8	12	16	20	24	28	32	36	40	44	48
5	10	15	20	25	30	35	40	45	50	55	60
6	12	18	24	30	36	42	48	54	60	66	72
7	14	21	28	35	42	49	56	63	70	77	84
8	16	24	32	40	48	56	64	72	80	88	96
9	18	27	36	45	54	63	72	81	90	99	108
10	20	30	40	50	60	70	80	90	100	110	120
11	22	33	44	55	66	77	88	99	110	121	132
12	24	36	48	60	72	84	96	108	120	132	144

Multiples of 3

1	2	3	4	5	6	7	8	9	10	11	12
2	4	6	8	10	12	14	16	18	20	22	24
3	6	9	12	15	18	21	24	27	30	33	36
4	8	12	16	20	24	28	32	36	40	44	48
5	10	15	20	25	30	35	40	45	50	55	60
6	12	18	24	30	36	42	48	54	60	66	72
7	14	21	28	35	42	49	56	63	70	77	84
8	16	24	32	40	48	56	64	72	80	88	96
9	18	27	36	45	54	63	72	81	90	99	108
10	20	30	40	50	60	70	80	90	100	110	120
11	22	33	44	55	66	77	88	99	110	121	132
12	24	36	48	60	72	84	96	108	120	132	144

Multiples of 4

1	2	3	4	5	6	7	8	9	10	11	12
2	4	6	8	10	12	14	16	18	20	22	24
3	6	9	12	15	18	21	24	27	30	33	36
4	8	12	16	20	24	28	32	36	40	44	48
5	10	15	20	25	30	35	40	45	50	55	60
6	12	18	24	30	36	42	48	54	60	66	72
7	14	21	28	35	42	49	56	63	70	77	84
8	16	24	32	40	48	56	64	72	80	88	96
9	18	27	36	45	54	63	72	81	90	99	108
10	20	30	40	50	60	70	80	90	100	110	120
11	22	33	44	55	66	77	88	99	110	121	132
12	24	36	48	60	72	84	96	108	120	132	144

Multiples of 5

1	2	3	4	5	6	7	8	9	10	11	12
2	4	6	8	10	12	14	16	18	20	22	24
3	6	9	12	15	18	21	24	27	30	33	36
4	8	12	16	20	24	28	32	36	40	44	48
5	10	15	20	25	30	35	40	45	50	55	60
6	12	18	24	30	36	42	48	54	60	66	72
7	14	21	28	35	42	49	56	63	70	77	84
8	16	24	32	40	48	56	64	72	80	88	96
9	18	27	36	45	54	63	72	81	90	99	108
10	20	30	40	50	60	70	80	90	100	110	120
11	22	33	44	55	66	77	88	99	110	121	132
12	24	36	48	60	72	84	96	108	120	132	144

Multiples of 6

1	2	3	4	5	6	7	8	9	10	11	12
2	4	6	8	10	12	14	16	18	20	22	24
3	6	9	12	15	18	21	24	27	30	33	36
4	8	12	16	20	24	28	32	36	40	44	48
5	10	15	20	25	30	35	40	45	50	55	60
6	12	18	24	30	36	42	48	54	60	66	72
7	14	21	28	35	42	49	56	63	70	77	84
8	16	24	32	40	48	56	64	72	80	88	96
9	18	27	36	45	54	63	72	81	90	99	108
10	20	30	40	50	60	70	80	90	100	110	120
11	22	33	44	55	66	77	88	99	110	121	132
12	24	36	48	60	72	84	96	108	120	132	144

Multiples of 7

1	2	3	4	5	6	7	8	9	10	11	12
2	4	6	8	10	12	14	16	18	20	22	24
3	6	9	12	15	18	21	24	27	30	33	36
4	8	12	16	20	24	28	32	36	40	44	48
5	10	15	20	25	30	35	40	45	50	55	60
6	12	18	24	30	36	42	48	54	60	66	72
7	14	21	28	35	42	49	56	63	70	77	84
8	16	24	32	40	48	56	64	72	80	88	96
9	18	27	36	45	54	63	72	81	90	99	108
10	20	30	40	50	60	70	80	90	100	110	120
11	22	33	44	55	66	77	88	99	110	121	132
12	24	36	48	60	72	84	96	108	120	132	144

Multiples of 8

1	2	3	4	5	6	7	8	9	10	11	12
2	4	6	8	10	12	14	16	18	20	22	24
3	6	9	12	15	18	21	24	27	30	33	36
4	8	12	16	20	24	28	32	36	40	44	48
5	10	15	20	25	30	35	40	45	50	55	60
6	12	18	24	30	36	42	48	54	60	66	72
7	14	21	28	35	42	49	56	63	70	77	84
8	16	24	32	40	48	56	64	72	80	88	96
9	18	27	36	45	54	63	72	81	90	99	108
10	20	30	40	50	60	70	80	90	100	110	120
11	22	33	44	55	66	77	88	99	110	121	132
12	24	36	48	60	72	84	96	108	120	132	144

Multiples of 9

1	2	3	4	5	6	7	8	9	10	11	12
2	4	6	8	10	12	14	16	18	20	22	24
3	6	9	12	15	18	21	24	27	30	33	36
4	8	12	16	20	24	28	32	36	40	44	48
5	10	15	20	25	30	35	40	45	50	55	60
6	12	18	24	30	36	42	48	54	60	66	72
7	14	21	28	35	42	49	56	63	70	77	84
8	16	24	32	40	48	56	64	72	80	88	96
9	18	27	36	45	54	63	72	81	90	99	108
10	20	30	40	50	60	70	80	90	100	110	120
11	22	33	44	55	66	77	88	99	110	121	132
12	24	36	48	60	72	84	96	108	120	132	144

Understanding Multiplication Across the Grades

Multiples of 10

1	2	3	4	5	6	7	8	9	10	11	12
2	4	6	8	10	12	14	16	18	20	22	24
3	6	9	12	15	18	21	24	27	30	33	36
4	8	12	16	20	24	28	32	36	40	44	48
5	10	15	20	25	30	35	40	45	50	55	60
6	12	18	24	30	36	42	48	54	60	66	72
7	14	21	28	35	42	49	56	63	70	77	84
8	16	24	32	40	48	56	64	72	80	88	96
9	18	27	36	45	54	63	72	81	90	99	108
10	20	30	40	50	60	70	80	90	100	110	120
11	22	33	44	55	66	77	88	99	110	121	132
12	24	36	48	60	72	84	96	108	120	132	144

Multiples of 12

1	2	3	4	5	6	7	8	9	10	11	12
2	4	6	8	10	12	14	16	18	20	22	24
3	6	9	12	15	18	21	24	27	30	33	36
4	8	12	16	20	24	28	32	36	40	44	48
5	10	15	20	25	30	35	40	45	50	55	60
6	12	18	24	30	36	42	48	54	60	66	72
7	14	21	28	35	42	49	56	63	70	77	84
8	16	24	32	40	48	56	64	72	80	88	96
9	18	27	36	45	54	63	72	81	90	99	108
10	20	30	40	50	60	70	80	90	100	110	120
11	22	33	44	55	66	77	88	99	110	121	132
12	24	36	48	60	72	84	96	108	120	132	144

Multiples of _____

1	2	3	4	5	6	7	8	9	10	11	12
2	4	6	8	10	12	14	16	18	20	22	24
3	6	9	12	15	18	21	24	27	30	33	36
4	8	12	16	20	24	28	32	36	40	44	48
5	10	15	20	25	30	35	40	45	50	55	60
6	12	18	24	30	36	42	48	54	60	66	72
7	14	21	28	35	42	49	56	63	70	77	84
8	16	24	32	40	48	56	64	72	80	88	96
9	18	27	36	45	54	63	72	81	90	99	108
10	20	30	40	50	60	70	80	90	100	110	120
11	22	33	44	55	66	77	88	99	110	121	132
12	24	36	48	60	72	84	96	108	120	132	144

Math Notes (3)

A Triangular Numbers Pattern Discovery

SAY *Students in one fifth-grade class that had been studying patterns and functions for about six weeks early in the year, said to their teacher, "Look what's happening!" Do you know what they might have been seeing?*

Expect this response:

✔ Expect someone to notice symmetry in the remaining numbers on the table. Acknowledge this discovery but reply that this is not what the students saw.

SAY *They said things like, "It's the ice cream cone problem," which is: Baskin Robbins has 31 flavors of ice cream. How many different double-scoop cones can they make? Others said, "It's the hand-shake problem." Which is, how many handshakes would occur if we all stood up and shook hands with each other? Other children said, "It's triangular numbers!" Do you see what they are seeing?*

Expect this response:

✔ Many in the audience will shake their heads "no."

SAY *If you're not familiar with triangular numbers, they are part of a very important sequence of numbers. It's easy to generate triangular numbers by arranging dots into a triangular pattern.*

Demonstrate triangular numbers 1, 3, 6, 10, 15, placing rows of dots in a triangular arrangement.

SAY *With one row of dots, we have one dot* (record a 1 to the side).

SAY *With two rows, there are three dots* (record a 3 under the 1).

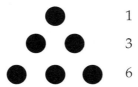

SAY *And, with three rows there are six dots* (record a 6 under the 3).

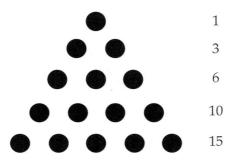

Continue process of adding rows and recording the number of dots up to five rows and fifteen dots.

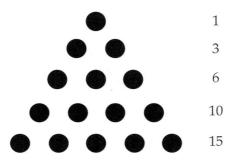

Do you notice what they were seeing?

Expect this response:

✔ Expect that some will still say, "no."

SAY *The number of facts that we have left to learn shows triangular numbers going backward. If that's the case, then after they learn their 4s, and you'll notice there are not many 4s left to learn, how many facts will they have left to learn?*

Record 3 on the transparency.

References

Burns, Marilyn. 2001. *Teaching Arithmetic: Lessons for Introducing Multiplication, Grade 3*. Sausalito, CA: Math Solutions Publications.

Burns, Marilyn. 1993. *A Collection of Math Lessons, Grades 3–6*. Sausalito, CA: Math Solutions Publications.

Overhead Transparency Masters (English)

Workshop Goals

Participants will:

◆ understand what it means to
teach multiplication for
understanding

◆ experience drill and practice in an
engaging problem-solving
context

◆ understand the distinction
between knowing multiplication
facts and simply memorizing
them

Workshop Agenda

◆ Welcome, Introduction, and Goals

◆ Multiplication Facts and Concepts

- Circles and Stars
- Multiplication Rectangles
- Building a Multiplication Table
- Designs Found in Multiples

◆ Working Toward Fluency: Patterns in the Multiplication Table

◆ What About Drill and Practice?

- Multiplication Tic-Tac-Toe
- Brian Bangel

◆ Reflect on Goals

Circles and Stars—Data Collection

1 ||||| /
2 ||||| ||||| /
3 ||||| |||||
4 ||||| ||||| ||||| ////
5 ||||| ||||| /
6 ||||| ||||| ||||| ||||| /
7
8 ||||| |||||
9 ||||| /
10 ||||| ||||| /
11
12 ||||| ||||| ||||| ||||| |||||
13
14
15 ||||| |||||
16 ////
17
18 ||||| ||||| ////

19
20 ||||| ||||| //
21
22
23
24 ||||| ||||| //
25 ||||| /
26
27
28
29
30 ||||| ////
31
32
33
34
35
36 ||||| ////

Blank Grid

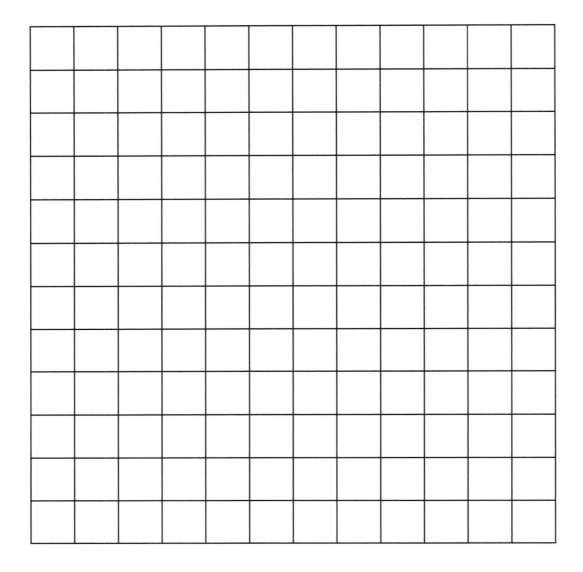

Multiplication Chart

×	1	2	3	4	5	6	7	8	9	10
1	1	2	3	4	5	6	7	8	9	10
2	2	4	6	8	10	12	14	16	18	20
3	3	6	9	12	15	18	21	24	27	30
4	4	8	12	16	20	24	28	32	36	40
5	5	10	15	20	25	30	35	40	45	50
6	6	12	18	24	30	36	42	48	54	60
7	7	14	21	28	35	42	49	56	63	70
8	8	16	24	32	40	48	56	64	72	80
9	9	18	27	36	45	54	63	72	81	90
10	10	20	30	40	50	60	70	80	90	100

Zero to Ninety-Nine Chart

0	1	2	3	4	5	6	7	8	9
10	11	12	13	14	15	16	17	18	19
20	21	22	23	24	25	26	27	28	29
30	31	32	33	34	35	36	37	38	39
40	41	42	43	44	45	46	47	48	49
50	51	52	53	54	55	56	57	58	59
60	61	62	63	64	65	66	67	68	69
70	71	72	73	74	75	76	77	78	79
80	81	82	83	84	85	86	87	88	89
90	91	92	93	94	95	96	97	98	99

Understanding Multiplication Across the Grades

Tic-Tac-Toe Products

1	2	3	4	5	6
7	8	9	10	12	14
15	16	18	20	21	24
25	27	28	30	32	35
36	40	42	45	48	49
54	56	63	64	72	81

1 2 3 4 5 6 7 8 9

Multiplication Table

1	2	3	4	5	6	7	8	9	10	11	12
2	4	6	8	10	12	14	16	18	20	22	24
3	6	9	12	15	18	21	24	27	30	33	36
4	8	12	16	20	24	28	32	36	40	44	48
5	10	15	20	25	30	35	40	45	50	55	60
6	12	18	24	30	36	42	48	54	60	66	72
7	14	21	28	35	42	49	56	63	70	77	84
8	16	24	32	40	48	56	64	72	80	88	96
9	18	27	36	45	54	63	72	81	90	99	108
10	20	30	40	50	60	70	80	90	100	110	120
11	22	33	44	55	66	77	88	99	110	121	132
12	24	36	48	60	72	84	96	108	120	132	144

Does How We Teach Multiplication Matter?

One presents math as a series of facts and procedures to be memorized.

vs.

The other presents math as relationships to be understood.

One gives the message that math is to be done quickly, with little thinking involved.

vs.

The other teaches the value of persistence in the search for math relationships.

One emphasizes skills in isolation, and presents math as a series of discrete, separate, and unrelated ideas.

vs.

The other emphasizes the interrelatedness of math ideas and skills developed in the context of their use.

One results in all too many children and adults who learn that math and in particular multiplication is a subject to be feared and avoided.

vs.

The other teaches children a love of mathematics and a fascination with the patterns that are revealed through its study.

One prepares children to do little more than compete with machines, and results in adults who are unable to determine if information coming from machines makes sense.

vs.

The other prepares children to use mathematics to make sense of complex situations in our technological world.

One approach results in children who may or may not know their multiplication tables.

vs.

The other teaches . . .

Workshop Handout Masters (English)

What Can Parents Do . . .

	. . . as an Adult?	. . . as a Parent?	. . . with Your Child at Home?	. . . for Your Child at School?
Parent as a Learner	• continue to learn and be a learner of mathematics • recognize that mathematics is an important tool for making sense of the world around you • recognize that new discoveries are still being made in mathematics	• learn what math is all about for your child • pay attention to experiences that impact your child's attitudes about mathematics	• investigate and play with numbers • involve your child in the measuring and comparing that you do at home • use games to support mathematical thinking • do mental arithmetic and share strategies	• attend parent math nights • look for information that comes home about your school's mathematics program • become familiar with mathematics as it is taught in your child's classroom
Parent as a Researcher	• be curious about how you and others solve problems • broaden your understanding of what mathematics is • find out about current research in mathematics teaching and learning	• ask questions to understand your child's thinking • be curious about how your child solves problems	• investigate with your child his or her mathematical questions • explore with your child the best time and place to do homework	• ask questions about your child's mathematics program, both the goals and how it is taught • find out about roles for parents in the mathematics program at your child's school
Parent as a Communicator	• recognize that learning and understanding mathematics depends on communication (listening, talking, and writing) • learn to examine and explain your own thinking	• share information with your child about how you use mathematics • display a positive disposition about mathematics	• talk with your child about the importance of mathematics in his or her life • explore the many ways to approach solving problems • be clear about your expectations for homework • find ways to show enthusiasm about mathematics	• find a way to let the school know what you want for your child's mathematical education • become a knowledgeable advocate for good mathematics education

Mathematically Powerful Students

- ◆ understand the power of mathematics as a tool for making sense of situations, information, and events in their world
- ◆ are persistent in their search for solutions to complex, "messy," or "ill-defined" tasks
- ◆ enjoy doing mathematics and find the pursuit of solutions to complex problems both challenging and engaging
- ◆ understand mathematics, not just arithmetic
- ◆ make connections within and among mathematical ideas and domains
- ◆ have a disposition to search for patterns and relationships;
- ◆ make conjectures and pursue finding out
- ◆ have "number sense" and are able to make sense of numerical information
- ◆ use algorithmic thinking and are able to estimate and mentally compute
- ◆ are able to work both independently and collaboratively as problem posers and problem solvers
- ◆ are able to communicate and justify their thinking and ideas both orally and in writing
- ◆ use tools available to them to solve problems and to examine mathematical ideas

The goal of mathematics education should be to produce learners who are both mathematically competent and confident. Mathematical competence does not come from memorizing rules and procedures. It comes from understanding mathematical relationships so that you can recognize those relationships and use them to make sense of information, situations, and problems that you encounter. Mathematical confidence comes from knowing that you understand mathematics and its beauty and utility, and from knowing that with persistence and, when appropriate, collaboration with others, you can make sense of information and situations you encounter, and you can solve even complex and messy or ill-defined problems.

From *Understanding Multiplication Across the Grades*. 2006. Portsmouth, NH: Heinemann.

Multiples of 2

1	2	3	4	5	6	7	8	9	10	11	12
2	4	6	8	10	12	14	16	18	20	22	24
3	6	9	12	15	18	21	24	27	30	33	36
4	8	12	16	20	24	28	32	36	40	44	48
5	10	15	20	25	30	35	40	45	50	55	60
6	12	18	24	30	36	42	48	54	60	66	72
7	14	21	28	35	42	49	56	63	70	77	84
8	16	24	32	40	48	56	64	72	80	88	96
9	18	27	36	45	54	63	72	81	90	99	108
10	20	30	40	50	60	70	80	90	100	110	120
11	22	33	44	55	66	77	88	99	110	121	132
12	24	36	48	60	72	84	96	108	120	132	144

Multiples of 3

1	2	3	4	5	6	7	8	9	10	11	12
2	4	6	8	10	12	14	16	18	20	22	24
3	6	9	12	15	18	21	24	27	30	33	36
4	8	12	16	20	24	28	32	36	40	44	48
5	10	15	20	25	30	35	40	45	50	55	60
6	12	18	24	30	36	42	48	54	60	66	72
7	14	21	28	35	42	49	56	63	70	77	84
8	16	24	32	40	48	56	64	72	80	88	96
9	18	27	36	45	54	63	72	81	90	99	108
10	20	30	40	50	60	70	80	90	100	110	120
11	22	33	44	55	66	77	88	99	110	121	132
12	24	36	48	60	72	84	96	108	120	132	144

Multiples of 4

1	2	3	4	5	6	7	8	9	10	11	12
2	4	6	8	10	12	14	16	18	20	22	24
3	6	9	12	15	18	21	24	27	30	33	36
4	8	12	16	20	24	28	32	36	40	44	48
5	10	15	20	25	30	35	40	45	50	55	60
6	12	18	24	30	36	42	48	54	60	66	72
7	14	21	28	35	42	49	56	63	70	77	84
8	16	24	32	40	48	56	64	72	80	88	96
9	18	27	36	45	54	63	72	81	90	99	108
10	20	30	40	50	60	70	80	90	100	110	120
11	22	33	44	55	66	77	88	99	110	121	132
12	24	36	48	60	72	84	96	108	120	132	144

Multiples of 5

1	2	3	4	5	6	7	8	9	10	11	12
2	4	6	8	10	12	14	16	18	20	22	24
3	6	9	12	15	18	21	24	27	30	33	36
4	8	12	16	20	24	28	32	36	40	44	48
5	10	15	20	25	30	35	40	45	50	55	60
6	12	18	24	30	36	42	48	54	60	66	72
7	14	21	28	35	42	49	56	63	70	77	84
8	16	24	32	40	48	56	64	72	80	88	96
9	18	27	36	45	54	63	72	81	90	99	108
10	20	30	40	50	60	70	80	90	100	110	120
11	22	33	44	55	66	77	88	99	110	121	132
12	24	36	48	60	72	84	96	108	120	132	144

(Handout 3 continues)

Multiples of 6

1	2	3	4	5	6	7	8	9	10	11	12
2	4	6	8	10	12	14	16	18	20	22	24
3	6	9	12	15	18	21	24	27	30	33	36
4	8	12	16	20	24	28	32	36	40	44	48
5	10	15	20	25	30	35	40	45	50	55	60
6	12	18	24	30	36	42	48	54	60	66	72
7	14	21	28	35	42	49	56	63	70	77	84
8	16	24	32	40	48	56	64	72	80	88	96
9	18	27	36	45	54	63	72	81	90	99	108
10	20	30	40	50	60	70	80	90	100	110	120
11	22	33	44	55	66	77	88	99	110	121	132
12	24	36	48	60	72	84	96	108	120	132	144

Multiples of 7

1	2	3	4	5	6	7	8	9	10	11	12
2	4	6	8	10	12	14	16	18	20	22	24
3	6	9	12	15	18	21	24	27	30	33	36
4	8	12	16	20	24	28	32	36	40	44	48
5	10	15	20	25	30	35	40	45	50	55	60
6	12	18	24	30	36	42	48	54	60	66	72
7	14	21	28	35	42	49	56	63	70	77	84
8	16	24	32	40	48	56	64	72	80	88	96
9	18	27	36	45	54	63	72	81	90	99	108
10	20	30	40	50	60	70	80	90	100	110	120
11	22	33	44	55	66	77	88	99	110	121	132
12	24	36	48	60	72	84	96	108	120	132	144

Multiples of 8

1	2	3	4	5	6	7	8	9	10	11	12
2	4	6	8	10	12	14	16	18	20	22	24
3	6	9	12	15	18	21	24	27	30	33	36
4	8	12	16	20	24	28	32	36	40	44	48
5	10	15	20	25	30	35	40	45	50	55	60
6	12	18	24	30	36	42	48	54	60	66	72
7	14	21	28	35	42	49	56	63	70	77	84
8	16	24	32	40	48	56	64	72	80	88	96
9	18	27	36	45	54	63	72	81	90	99	108
10	20	30	40	50	60	70	80	90	100	110	120
11	22	33	44	55	66	77	88	99	110	121	132
12	24	36	48	60	72	84	96	108	120	132	144

Multiples of 9

1	2	3	4	5	6	7	8	9	10	11	12
2	4	6	8	10	12	14	16	18	20	22	24
3	6	9	12	15	18	21	24	27	30	33	36
4	8	12	16	20	24	28	32	36	40	44	48
5	10	15	20	25	30	35	40	45	50	55	60
6	12	18	24	30	36	42	48	54	60	66	72
7	14	21	28	35	42	49	56	63	70	77	84
8	16	24	32	40	48	56	64	72	80	88	96
9	18	27	36	45	54	63	72	81	90	99	108
10	20	30	40	50	60	70	80	90	100	110	120
11	22	33	44	55	66	77	88	99	110	121	132
12	24	36	48	60	72	84	96	108	120	132	144

(Handout 3 continues)

Understanding Multiplication Across the Grades

Multiples of 10

1	2	3	4	5	6	7	8	9	10	11	12
2	4	6	8	10	12	14	16	18	20	22	24
3	6	9	12	15	18	21	24	27	30	33	36
4	8	12	16	20	24	28	32	36	40	44	48
5	10	15	20	25	30	35	40	45	50	55	60
6	12	18	24	30	36	42	48	54	60	66	72
7	14	21	28	35	42	49	56	63	70	77	84
8	16	24	32	40	48	56	64	72	80	88	96
9	18	27	36	45	54	63	72	81	90	99	108
10	20	30	40	50	60	70	80	90	100	110	120
11	22	33	44	55	66	77	88	99	110	121	132
12	24	36	48	60	72	84	96	108	120	132	144

Multiples of 11

1	2	3	4	5	6	7	8	9	10	11	12
2	4	6	8	10	12	14	16	18	20	22	24
3	6	9	12	15	18	21	24	27	30	33	36
4	8	12	16	20	24	28	32	36	40	44	48
5	10	15	20	25	30	35	40	45	50	55	60
6	12	18	24	30	36	42	48	54	60	66	72
7	14	21	28	35	42	49	56	63	70	77	84
8	16	24	32	40	48	56	64	72	80	88	96
9	18	27	36	45	54	63	72	81	90	99	108
10	20	30	40	50	60	70	80	90	100	110	120
11	22	33	44	55	66	77	88	99	110	121	132
12	24	36	48	60	72	84	96	108	120	132	144

Multiples of 12

1	2	3	4	5	6	7	8	9	10	11	12
2	4	6	8	10	12	14	16	18	20	22	24
3	6	9	12	15	18	21	24	27	30	33	36
4	8	12	16	20	24	28	32	36	40	44	48
5	10	15	20	25	30	35	40	45	50	55	60
6	12	18	24	30	36	42	48	54	60	66	72
7	14	21	28	35	42	49	56	63	70	77	84
8	16	24	32	40	48	56	64	72	80	88	96
9	18	27	36	45	54	63	72	81	90	99	108
10	20	30	40	50	60	70	80	90	100	110	120
11	22	33	44	55	66	77	88	99	110	121	132
12	24	36	48	60	72	84	96	108	120	132	144

Multiples of _____

1	2	3	4	5	6	7	8	9	10	11	12
2	4	6	8	10	12	14	16	18	20	22	24
3	6	9	12	15	18	21	24	27	30	33	36
4	8	12	16	20	24	28	32	36	40	44	48
5	10	15	20	25	30	35	40	45	50	55	60
6	12	18	24	30	36	42	48	54	60	66	72
7	14	21	28	35	42	49	56	63	70	77	84
8	16	24	32	40	48	56	64	72	80	88	96
9	18	27	36	45	54	63	72	81	90	99	108
10	20	30	40	50	60	70	80	90	100	110	120
11	22	33	44	55	66	77	88	99	110	121	132
12	24	36	48	60	72	84	96	108	120	132	144

Multiplication Chart

×	1	2	3	4	5	6	7	8	9	10
1	1	2	3	4	5	6	7	8	9	10
2	2	4	6	8	10	12	14	16	18	20
3	3	6	9	12	15	18	21	24	27	30
4	4	8	12	16	20	24	28	32	36	40
5	5	10	15	20	25	30	35	40	45	50
6	6	12	18	24	30	36	42	48	54	60
7	7	14	21	28	35	42	49	56	63	70
8	8	16	24	32	40	48	56	64	72	80
9	9	18	27	36	45	54	63	72	81	90
10	10	20	30	40	50	60	70	80	90	100

Understanding Multiplication Across the Grades

Zero to Ninety-Nine Chart

0	1	2	3	4	5	6	7	8	9
10	11	12	13	14	15	16	17	18	19
20	21	22	23	24	25	26	27	28	29
30	31	32	33	34	35	36	37	38	39
40	41	42	43	44	45	46	47	48	49
50	51	52	53	54	55	56	57	58	59
60	61	62	63	64	65	66	67	68	69
70	71	72	73	74	75	76	77	78	79
80	81	82	83	84	85	86	87	88	89
90	91	92	93	94	95	96	97	98	99

Tic-Tac-Toe Products

Object

Be the first team to get four products in a row (horizontally, vertically, or diagonally).

Divide into two teams (Xs and Os).

1. Team X selects two factors by placing a marker on the numbers (1–9) to multiply. The product is marked by placing an X on the grid.

2. Team O then moves one marker to make a new product and places an O on the grid.

3. Teams alternate moving one marker at a time and continue placing Xs and Os until a team has marked four products in a row.

4. After several games, players should discuss their strategies.

Understanding Multiplication Across the Grades

Tic-Tac-Toe Products

1	2	3	4	5	6
7	8	9	10	12	14
15	16	18	20	21	24
25	27	28	30	32	35
36	40	42	45	48	49
54	56	63	64	72	81

1   2   3   4   5   6   7   8   9

Does How We Teach Multiplication Matter?

One presents math as a series of facts and procedures to be memorized.   vs.   The other presents math as relationships to be understood.

One gives the message that math is to be done quickly, with little thinking involved.   vs.   The other teaches the value of persistence in the search for math relationships.

One emphasizes skills in isolation, and presents math as a series of discrete, separate, and unrelated ideas.   vs.   The other emphasizes the interrelatedness of math ideas and skills developed in the context of their use.

One results in all too many children and adults who learn that math and in particular multiplication is a subject to be feared and avoided.   vs.   The other teaches children a love of mathematics and a fascination with the patterns that are revealed through its study.

One prepares children to do little more than compete with machines, and results in adults who are unable to determine if information coming from machines makes sense.   vs.   The other prepares children to use mathematics to make sense of complex situations in our technological world.

One approach results in
children who may or may
not know their multiplication
tables.

vs.

The other teaches . . .

Resource Texts
Referenced in Workshop

Math by All Means and *Teaching Arithmetic* 2–4 by Marilyn Burns. These multiweek units focus on geometry, place value, multiplication, division, probability, and money.

A Collection of Math Lessons from Grades 3–6 by Marilyn Burns. This is the source of the multiplication lessons with rectangles and patterns in the multiplication tables.

Developing Number Concepts by Kathy Richardson. This series of books (and the reference that follows) focuses on building young children's fluency with numbers.

Math Time: The Learning Environment by Kathy Richardson.

Mathematical Power: Lessons from a Classroom by Ruth Parker and the result of her year as a researcher in a fifth-grade classroom. It addresses the need for complex changes in math teaching and follows a teacher working to make those changes.

Seeing Fractions by Susan Jo Russell and Rebecca Corwin. This 6- to 8-week unit on fractions is appropriate for grades 4–6 and illustrates what a good math curriculum can look like. It's now incorporated into the K–5 series *Investigations in Number, Data, Space*.

Why Numbers Count: Quantitative Literacy for Tomorrow's America by Lynn A. Steen. This book overviews the need for changes in children's understanding of numbers.

Other Quality Mathematics Resources for Parents

About Teaching Mathematics by Marilyn Burns. This book is a rich resource for great problems across the strands of mathematics.

Beyond Facts and Flashcards: Exploring Math with Your Kids by Jan Mokros. This book suggests many practical, everyday ways of exploring mathematics as a family.

Family Math by the Lawrence Hall of Science.

The I Hate Math Book and *Math for Smarty Pants*, both by Marilyn Burns and full of fun math problems to work on as a family.

Professional Resources That Address Issues in Mathematics Education

On the Shoulders of Giants, edited by Lynn Arthur Steen.

Principles and Standards for School Mathematics by the National Council of Teachers of Mathematics.

Thinking Mathematically by Leone Burton. It will engage you in thinking about yourself as a mathematical problem solver.

Research Brief

National Research Council. (2001). *Adding It Up: Helping Children Learn Mathematics.* J. Kilpatrick, J. Swafford, and B. Findell (Eds.). Mathematics Learning Study Committee, Center for Education, Division of Behavioral and Social Sciences and Education, Washington, DC: National Academy Press. www.nap.edu

Excerpts: This report was "approved by the Governing Board of the National Research Council, whose members are drawn from the Councils of the National Academy of Sciences, the National Academy of Engineering, and the Institute of Medicine. The members of the committee responsible for the report were chosen for their special competencies with regard for appropriate balance." They were given the following charge:

- to synthesize the rich and diverse research on prekindergarten through eighth-grade mathematics learning

- to provide research-based recommendations for teaching, teacher education, and curriculum for improving student learning and to identify areas where research is needed

- to give advice and guidance to educators, researchers, publishers, policy makers, and parents

Adding It Up addresses many questions: What exactly do we know from research about the teaching and learning of mathematics? And what does this research really tell us? Should children learn computation methods before they understand the concepts? What is the role of concrete manipulatives? Do teacher and student expectations make a difference? The conclusions and recommendations drawn from this report of the research provide us with information about improving the teaching and learning of mathematics.

Selected quotes:

> The more mathematical concepts they (students) understand, the more sensible mathematics becomes. In contrast, when students are seldom given challenging mathematical problems to solve, they come to expect that memorizing rather than sense-making paves the road to learning mathematics. (p. 131)

> It seems clear that instruction focused solely on symbolic manipulation without understanding is ineffective for most students. It is necessary to correct that imbalance by paying more attention to conceptual understanding as well as the other strands of proficiency and by helping students connect them. (p. 241)

> By focusing on ways to use the elementary and middle school curriculum to support the development of algebraic reasoning, these efforts attempt to avoid difficulties many students now experience and to lay a better foundation for secondary school mathematics. From the earliest grades of elementary school, students can be acquiring the rudiments of algebra, particularly its representational aspect. (p. 280)

Mid-continent Research for Education and Learning. (2002). *EDThoughts, What We Know About Mathematics Teaching and Learning.* **J. Sutton & A. Krueger (Eds.).**

Excerpts: This book summarizes educational research and surveys of best classroom practices and offers implications for improved teaching and learning. Addressing the many different questions related to mathematics education, it provides background for each from the perspective of research and best practice followed by implications for improving classroom instruction. Not only intended for teachers and administrators, this book recognizes that all stakeholder groups will need a common understanding of the current status of mathematics education and the direction that research and best practice indicate for improvement. "Every person concerned with teaching and learning mathematics, whether teacher, administrator, student, parent, or community member, will find useful information in this document."

Summary: What Do We Know About How Students Learn Mathematics?

> Students may have difficulty making the transition from arithmetic to algebra. Research indicates how the development of algebraic reasoning can be supported in elementary and middle school. Young students can learn algebra concepts, especially algebraic representation and the notion of variable and function, and basic concepts can be introduced as patterning and as a generalization of arithmetic. For example, patterns on a hundreds chart can be discovered and analyzed. (p. 76)

Washington State Office of the Superintendent of Public Instruction. (2000). *Teaching and Learning Mathematics: Using Research to Shift From the "Yesterday" Mind to the "Tomorrow" Mind.* **J. Johnson (Ed.).**

Excerpts: This book provides an overview of the potential and challenges of teaching quality mathematics (K–12). A good portion of it summarizes some of the research results, in a very concise format, related to each of the essential learning academic requirements in mathematics. It is a resource text designed to serve as a catalyst for promoting reflection, discussion, and problem solving within the education community and to help educators become knowledgeable about available research results and ways they can be integrated into the classroom. It is available at www.k12.wa.us.

Summary:

> Students learning multiplication as a conceptual operation need exposure to a variety of models (e.g., rectangular array, area). Access only to "multiplication as repeated addition" models and the term "times" leads to basic misunderstandings of multiplication that complicate future extensions of multiplication to decimals and fractions. (Bell, Greer, Mangan, and Grimison; and English and Halford, p. 9)

Summary:

> Student use of concrete materials in mathematical contexts helps both in the initial construction of correct concepts and procedures and in the retention and self-correction of these concepts and procedures through mental imagery. (Fuson, p. 43)

References

Bell, A., Greer, B., Mangan, C., and Grimison L. "Children's Performance on Multiplicative Word Problems: Elements of a Descriptive Theory." *Journal for Research In Mathematics Education,* 1989, 20(5): 434–449.

Fuson, K. "Mathematics Education, Elementary." In M. Alkin (Ed.), *Encyclopedia of Educational Research* (Sixth Ed., Vol. 3). New York: MacMillan, 1992c.

Feedback Form

Session Title: _____

Location: _____ Date: _____

1. What new ideas do you have as a result of this session?

2. What ideas from this session will you use with your child(ren)?

3. Overall, how would you rate this session?

     |_____|_____|_____|_____|

        Not   Extremely

    Informative   Informative

4. Is there anything else you would like us to know?

5. Would you like to be informed about any upcoming sessions? If so, please provide the following:

Name: _____

Address: _____

_____

_____

E-mail: _____

Overhead Transparency Masters (Spanish)

Metas para la Sesión

Los participantes:

◆ Entenderán lo que significa
enseñar la multiplicación de
manera que se entienda

◆ Experimentarán el ejercicio y la
práctica en un contexto interesante de resolución de problemas

◆ Entenderán la distinción entre
saber las hechos de multiplicar y
simplemente memorizarlas

Agenda del Taller

◆ Bienvenida, Presentación y Metas

◆ Hechos de Multiplicación y Conceptos

- Círculos y Estrellas
- Rectángulos de Multiplicación
- Construyendo una tabla de multiplicación
- Diseños encontrados en los múltiples

◆ Hacia la Fluidez: Patronas dentro de la tabla de multiplicación

◆ Y,¿de los ejercicios y la práctica?

- Productos del "Gato" (Tic-Tac-Toe Products)
- Brian Bangel

◆ Reflejar en las Metas

Círculos y Estrellas—Reunión de Datos

1	卌 /	19	
2	卌 卌 /	20	卌 卌 //
3	卌 卌	21	
4	卌 卌 卌 ////	22	
5	卌 卌 /	23	
6	卌 卌 卌 卌 /	24	卌 卌 //
7		25	卌 /
8	卌 卌	26	
9	卌 /	27	
10	卌 卌 /	28	
11		29	
12	卌 卌 卌 卌 卌	30	卌 ////
13		31	
14		32	
15	卌 卌	33	
16	////	34	
17		35	
18	卌 卌 ////	36	卌 ////

Tabla vacía

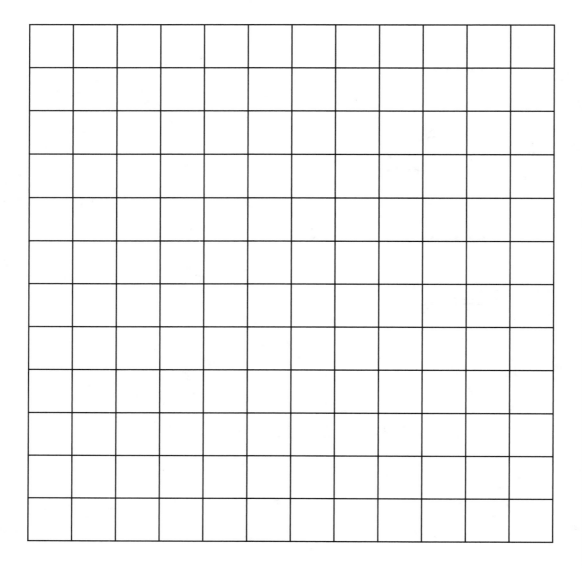

Understanding Multiplication Across the Grades

Diagrama de Multiplicación

×	1	2	3	4	5	6	7	8	9	10
1	1	2	3	4	5	6	7	8	9	10
2	2	4	6	8	10	12	14	16	18	20
3	3	6	9	12	15	18	21	24	27	30
4	4	8	12	16	20	24	28	32	36	40
5	5	10	15	20	25	30	35	40	45	50
6	6	12	18	24	30	36	42	48	54	60
7	7	14	21	28	35	42	49	56	63	70
8	8	16	24	32	40	48	56	64	72	80
9	9	18	27	36	45	54	63	72	81	90
10	10	20	30	40	50	60	70	80	90	100

Diagrama de Cero
a Noventa y Nueve

0	1	2	3	4	5	6	7	8	9
10	11	12	13	14	15	16	17	18	19
20	21	22	23	24	25	26	27	28	29
30	31	32	33	34	35	36	37	38	39
40	41	42	43	44	45	46	47	48	49
50	51	52	53	54	55	56	57	58	59
60	61	62	63	64	65	66	67	68	69
70	71	72	73	74	75	76	77	78	79
80	81	82	83	84	85	86	87	88	89
90	91	92	93	94	95	96	97	98	99

Productos del "Gato"

1	2	3	4	5	6
7	8	9	10	12	14
15	16	18	20	21	24
25	27	28	30	32	35
36	40	42	45	48	49
54	56	63	64	72	81

1 2 3 4 5 6 7 8 9

Tabla de Multiplicación

1	2	3	4	5	6	7	8	9	10	11	12
2	4	6	8	10	12	14	16	18	20	22	24
3	6	9	12	15	18	21	24	27	30	33	36
4	8	12	16	20	24	28	32	36	40	44	48
5	10	15	20	25	30	35	40	45	50	55	60
6	12	18	24	30	36	42	48	54	60	66	72
7	14	21	28	35	42	49	56	63	70	77	84
8	16	24	32	40	48	56	64	72	80	88	96
9	18	27	36	45	54	63	72	81	90	99	108
10	20	30	40	50	60	70	80	90	100	110	120
11	22	33	44	55	66	77	88	99	110	121	132
12	24	36	48	60	72	84	96	108	120	132	144

Understanding Multiplication Across the Grades

¿Importa cómo se enseñen las Matemáticas?

Una forma presenta las matemáticas como una serie de tablas y procedimientos que hay que memorizar	vs.	La otra presenta las matemáticas como relaciones que han de entenderse
Una forma da el mensaje de que las matemáticas se deben hacer con rapidez y con poco grado de razonamiento	vs.	La otra enseña el valor de la persistencia para buscar las relaciones matemáticas
Una forma enfatiza las destrezas de manera aislada y presenta las matemáticas como una serie de ideas discretas, separadas y sin relación	vs.	La otra enfatiza la interrelación de las ideas en las matemáticas y las destrezas que se crean en el contexto de su uso
Una forma tiene como resultado que muchos niños y adultos piensen que las matemáticas y en particular la multiplicación son algo que hay que temer y evitar	vs.	La otra enseña a los niños a amar las matemáticas y a fascinarse con los patrones que van descubriendo mediante su raíz
Una forma prepara a los niños poco menos que para competir con las calculadoras y como resultado, los adultos no son capaces de determinar si la información de la calculadora tiene sentido	vs.	La otra prepara a los niños a usar las matemáticas para encontrar sentido en las situaciones complejas de nuestro mundo tecnológico

Un enfoque tiene como resultado niños que pueden saber o no saber las tablas de multiplicar   vs.   El otro enfoque enseña . . .

Workshop
Handout
Masters
(Spanish)

Lo que los padres pueden hacer . . .				
	. . . ¿de adulto?	**. . . ¿de padre?**	**. . . ¿con su hijo en casa?**	**. . . ¿para su hijo en el colegio?**
Los padres como estudiantes	• continuen de aprender y sean estudiantes de matemáticas • reconozcan la importancia de matemáticas en el mundo actual • reconozcan que hay nuevos descubrimientos	• aprendan lo que son las matemáticas para su hijo • presten atención a las experiencas que influyan a su hijo y su actitud	• investiguen y jueguen con los números • incluyan a su hijo cuando midan o comparen en casa • usen juegos para apoyar el pensar de una manera de matemáticas • comparten información de una manera usando matemáticas	• asistan a las reuniones para padres e hijos de matemáticas • busquen información que llega a casa del programa de matemáticas • Busquen información que reciban del colegio del programa de matemática • conozca la manera en que enseñan matemáticas
Los padres como investigadores	• sean curiosos en cuanto a la manera suya de resolver problemas • amplíense la comprensión de matemáticas • entérense de las investigaciones actuales en cuanto a la enseñanza y el aprendizaje de matemáticas	• pregúntenle a su hijo para comprender su manera de pensar • sean curiosos en cuanto a la manera de su hijo de resolver problemas	• investigue con su hijo las preguntas que tiene • exploren con su hijo cuándo y dónde es mejor hacer la tarea	• pregunten del programa; las metas y como lo enseñan • entérense de lo que los padres pueden hacer en los programas en el colegio
Los padres como comunicadores	• reconozcan que el aprendizaje y la comprensión de matemáticas depende de la comunicación (el escuchar, el hablar y el escribir) • aprendan a examinar y explicar su propia manera de pensar	• comparten información con su hijo sobre la manera suya de usar matemáticas • sean positivos en cuanto a las matemáticas	• hablen con su hijo de la importancia de matemáticas en la vida actual • exploren las varias maneras de resolver problemas • sean claros en cuanto a sus expectativas para la tarea • encuentren maneras de mostrar ánimo para las matemáticas	• busquen una manera para que sepa el colegio lo que usted quiera para su hijo • lleguen a ser defensores de buenos programas

Los Alumnos Sólidos en Matemáticas. . . .

◆ Entienden el poder de las matemáticas como instrumento para encontrar sentido en las situaciones, información y eventos que suceden en el mundo;

◆ Son persistentes en su búsqueda de soluciones para tareas complejas, confusas o capciosas;

◆ Disfrutan las matemáticas y encuentran que la búsqueda de soluciones a los problemas complejos es difícil pero muy interesante;

◆ Entienden las matemáticas no solamente la aritmética;

◆ Encuentran relación en y entre las ideas matemáticas y las áreas que cubren;

◆ Tienen la disposición de buscar pautas y relaciones;

◆ Se hacen conjeturas y se dedican a indagar;

◆ Poseen "sentido de los números" y son capaces de encontrar sentido a la información numérica;

◆ Usan un pensamiento algorítmico y son capaces de estimar y calcular mentalmente;

◆ Son capaces de trabajar tanto en forma independiente como colaborativa como personas que plantean y resuelven problemas;

◆ Son capaces de comunicar y de justificar su pensamiento e ideas tanto en forma oral como escrita; y

◆ Usan los instrumentos disponibles para resolver problemas y examinar las ideas matemáticas.

La meta de la educación en matemáticas debe ser la de producir estudiantes que sean competentes y tengan confianza en el uso de las matemáticas. La aptitud matemática no surge de memorizar reglas y procedimientos, sino de entender las relaciones matemáticas para poder reconocer esas relaciones y usarlas con el fin de encontrar sentido en la información, situaciones y problemas que encuentres. La confianza matemática surge cuando sabes que entiendes la materia, así como su belleza y utilidad y te das cuenta de que con persistencia y, cuando es apropiado, con la colaboración de otros, puedes encontrar sentido en la información y las situaciones que encuentres y que puedes resolver incluso los problemas más complejos, confusos o capciosos.

From *Understanding Multiplication Across the Grades*. 2006. Portsmouth, NH: Heinemann.

Tablas de Multiplicación

Múltiples de 2

1	2	3	4	5	6	7	8	9	10	11	12
2	4	6	8	10	12	14	16	18	20	22	24
3	6	9	12	15	18	21	24	27	30	33	36
4	8	12	16	20	24	28	32	36	40	44	48
5	10	15	20	25	30	35	40	45	50	55	60
6	12	18	24	30	36	42	48	54	60	66	72
7	14	21	28	35	42	49	56	63	70	77	84
8	16	24	32	40	48	56	64	72	80	88	96
9	18	27	36	45	54	63	72	81	90	99	108
10	20	30	40	50	60	70	80	90	100	110	120
11	22	33	44	55	66	77	88	99	110	121	132
12	24	36	48	60	72	84	96	108	120	132	144

Múltiples de 3

1	2	3	4	5	6	7	8	9	10	11	12
2	4	6	8	10	12	14	16	18	20	22	24
3	6	9	12	15	18	21	24	27	30	33	36
4	8	12	16	20	24	28	32	36	40	44	48
5	10	15	20	25	30	35	40	45	50	55	60
6	12	18	24	30	36	42	48	54	60	66	72
7	14	21	28	35	42	49	56	63	70	77	84
8	16	24	32	40	48	56	64	72	80	88	96
9	18	27	36	45	54	63	72	81	90	99	108
10	20	30	40	50	60	70	80	90	100	110	120
11	22	33	44	55	66	77	88	99	110	121	132
12	24	36	48	60	72	84	96	108	120	132	144

Múltiples de 4

1	2	3	4	5	6	7	8	9	10	11	12
2	4	6	8	10	12	14	16	18	20	22	24
3	6	9	12	15	18	21	24	27	30	33	36
4	8	12	16	20	24	28	32	36	40	44	48
5	10	15	20	25	30	35	40	45	50	55	60
6	12	18	24	30	36	42	48	54	60	66	72
7	14	21	28	35	42	49	56	63	70	77	84
8	16	24	32	40	48	56	64	72	80	88	96
9	18	27	36	45	54	63	72	81	90	99	108
10	20	30	40	50	60	70	80	90	100	110	120
11	22	33	44	55	66	77	88	99	110	121	132
12	24	36	48	60	72	84	96	108	120	132	144

Múltiples de 5

1	2	3	4	5	6	7	8	9	10	11	12
2	4	6	8	10	12	14	16	18	20	22	24
3	6	9	12	15	18	21	24	27	30	33	36
4	8	12	16	20	24	28	32	36	40	44	48
5	10	15	20	25	30	35	40	45	50	55	60
6	12	18	24	30	36	42	48	54	60	66	72
7	14	21	28	35	42	49	56	63	70	77	84
8	16	24	32	40	48	56	64	72	80	88	96
9	18	27	36	45	54	63	72	81	90	99	108
10	20	30	40	50	60	70	80	90	100	110	120
11	22	33	44	55	66	77	88	99	110	121	132
12	24	36	48	60	72	84	96	108	120	132	144

Handout 3 continues

Múltiples de 6

1	2	3	4	5	6	7	8	9	10	11	12
2	4	6	8	10	12	14	16	18	20	22	24
3	6	9	12	15	18	21	24	27	30	33	36
4	8	12	16	20	24	28	32	36	40	44	48
5	10	15	20	25	30	35	40	45	50	55	60
6	12	18	24	30	36	42	48	54	60	66	72
7	14	21	28	35	42	49	56	63	70	77	84
8	16	24	32	40	48	56	64	72	80	88	96
9	18	27	36	45	54	63	72	81	90	99	108
10	20	30	40	50	60	70	80	90	100	110	120
11	22	33	44	55	66	77	88	99	110	121	132
12	24	36	48	60	72	84	96	108	120	132	144

Múltiples de 7

1	2	3	4	5	6	7	8	9	10	11	12
2	4	6	8	10	12	14	16	18	20	22	24
3	6	9	12	15	18	21	24	27	30	33	36
4	8	12	16	20	24	28	32	36	40	44	48
5	10	15	20	25	30	35	40	45	50	55	60
6	12	18	24	30	36	42	48	54	60	66	72
7	14	21	28	35	42	49	56	63	70	77	84
8	16	24	32	40	48	56	64	72	80	88	96
9	18	27	36	45	54	63	72	81	90	99	108
10	20	30	40	50	60	70	80	90	100	110	120
11	22	33	44	55	66	77	88	99	110	121	132
12	24	36	48	60	72	84	96	108	120	132	144

Múltiples de 8

1	2	3	4	5	6	7	8	9	10	11	12
2	4	6	8	10	12	14	16	18	20	22	24
3	6	9	12	15	18	21	24	27	30	33	36
4	8	12	16	20	24	28	32	36	40	44	48
5	10	15	20	25	30	35	40	45	50	55	60
6	12	18	24	30	36	42	48	54	60	66	72
7	14	21	28	35	42	49	56	63	70	77	84
8	16	24	32	40	48	56	64	72	80	88	96
9	18	27	36	45	54	63	72	81	90	99	108
10	20	30	40	50	60	70	80	90	100	110	120
11	22	33	44	55	66	77	88	99	110	121	132
12	24	36	48	60	72	84	96	108	120	132	144

Múltiples de 9

1	2	3	4	5	6	7	8	9	10	11	12
2	4	6	8	10	12	14	16	18	20	22	24
3	6	9	12	15	18	21	24	27	30	33	36
4	8	12	16	20	24	28	32	36	40	44	48
5	10	15	20	25	30	35	40	45	50	55	60
6	12	18	24	30	36	42	48	54	60	66	72
7	14	21	28	35	42	49	56	63	70	77	84
8	16	24	32	40	48	56	64	72	80	88	96
9	18	27	36	45	54	63	72	81	90	99	108
10	20	30	40	50	60	70	80	90	100	110	120
11	22	33	44	55	66	77	88	99	110	121	132
12	24	36	48	60	72	84	96	108	120	132	144

Handout 3 continues

Múltiples de 10

1	2	3	4	5	6	7	8	9	10	11	12
2	4	6	8	10	12	14	16	18	20	22	24
3	6	9	12	15	18	21	24	27	30	33	36
4	8	12	16	20	24	28	32	36	40	44	48
5	10	15	20	25	30	35	40	45	50	55	60
6	12	18	24	30	36	42	48	54	60	66	72
7	14	21	28	35	42	49	56	63	70	77	84
8	16	24	32	40	48	56	64	72	80	88	96
9	18	27	36	45	54	63	72	81	90	99	108
10	20	30	40	50	60	70	80	90	100	110	120
11	22	33	44	55	66	77	88	99	110	121	132
12	24	36	48	60	72	84	96	108	120	132	144

Múltiples de 11

1	2	3	4	5	6	7	8	9	10	11	12
2	4	6	8	10	12	14	16	18	20	22	24
3	6	9	12	15	18	21	24	27	30	33	36
4	8	12	16	20	24	28	32	36	40	44	48
5	10	15	20	25	30	35	40	45	50	55	60
6	12	18	24	30	36	42	48	54	60	66	72
7	14	21	28	35	42	49	56	63	70	77	84
8	16	24	32	40	48	56	64	72	80	88	96
9	18	27	36	45	54	63	72	81	90	99	108
10	20	30	40	50	60	70	80	90	100	110	120
11	22	33	44	55	66	77	88	99	110	121	132
12	24	36	48	60	72	84	96	108	120	132	144

Múltiples de 12

1	2	3	4	5	6	7	8	9	10	11	12
2	4	6	8	10	12	14	16	18	20	22	24
3	6	9	12	15	18	21	24	27	30	33	36
4	8	12	16	20	24	28	32	36	40	44	48
5	10	15	20	25	30	35	40	45	50	55	60
6	12	18	24	30	36	42	48	54	60	66	72
7	14	21	28	35	42	49	56	63	70	77	84
8	16	24	32	40	48	56	64	72	80	88	96
9	18	27	36	45	54	63	72	81	90	99	108
10	20	30	40	50	60	70	80	90	100	110	120
11	22	33	44	55	66	77	88	99	110	121	132
12	24	36	48	60	72	84	96	108	120	132	144

Múltiples de _____

1	2	3	4	5	6	7	8	9	10	11	12
2	4	6	8	10	12	14	16	18	20	22	24
3	6	9	12	15	18	21	24	27	30	33	36
4	8	12	16	20	24	28	32	36	40	44	48
5	10	15	20	25	30	35	40	45	50	55	60
6	12	18	24	30	36	42	48	54	60	66	72
7	14	21	28	35	42	49	56	63	70	77	84
8	16	24	32	40	48	56	64	72	80	88	96
9	18	27	36	45	54	63	72	81	90	99	108
10	20	30	40	50	60	70	80	90	100	110	120
11	22	33	44	55	66	77	88	99	110	121	132
12	24	36	48	60	72	84	96	108	120	132	144

Diagrama de Multiplicación

×	1	2	3	4	5	6	7	8	9	10
1	1	2	3	4	5	6	7	8	9	10
2	2	4	6	8	10	12	14	16	18	20
3	3	6	9	12	15	18	21	24	27	30
4	4	8	12	16	20	24	28	32	36	40
5	5	10	15	20	25	30	35	40	45	50
6	6	12	18	24	30	36	42	48	54	60
7	7	14	21	28	35	42	49	56	63	70
8	8	16	24	32	40	48	56	64	72	80
9	9	18	27	36	45	54	63	72	81	90
10	10	20	30	40	50	60	70	80	90	100

Diagrama de Cero
a Noventa y Nueve

0	1	2	3	4	5	6	7	8	9
10	11	12	13	14	15	16	17	18	19
20	21	22	23	24	25	26	27	28	29
30	31	32	33	34	35	36	37	38	39
40	41	42	43	44	45	46	47	48	49
50	51	52	53	54	55	56	57	58	59
60	61	62	63	64	65	66	67	68	69
70	71	72	73	74	75	76	77	78	79
80	81	82	83	84	85	86	87	88	89
90	91	92	93	94	95	96	97	98	99

Productos del "Gato"

Objeto

Sé el primer equipo que obtiene cuatro productos en una fila (horizontal, vertical o diagonalmente).

Divídanse en 2 equipos (Xs y Os)

1. El equipo O selecciona dos factores colocando un marcador en los números (1–9) para multiplicar. El producto se marca poniendo una O en la cuadrícula.

2. El equipo X puede mover un marcador para obtener un nuevo producto y colocar una X en la cuadrícula.

3. Los equipos alternan su turno de mover un marcador a la vez y continúan poniendo Xs y Os hasta que un equipo haya marcado cuatro productos de una fila.

4. Después de varios juegos, los jugadores deben discutir sus estrategias.

© 2006 by Mathematics Education Collaborative from *Understanding Multiplication Across the Grades*. Portsmouth, NH: Heinemann.

Productos del "Gato"

1	2	3	4	5	6
7	8	9	10	12	14
15	16	18	20	21	24
25	27	28	30	32	35
36	40	42	45	48	49
54	56	63	64	72	81

1 2 3 4 5 6 7 8 9

¿Importa cómo se enseñen las Matemáticas?

Una forma presenta las matemáticas como una serie de tablas y procedimientos que hay que memorizar	vs.	La otra presenta las matemáticas como relaciones que han de entenderse
Una forma da el mensaje de que las matemáticas se deben hacer con rapidez y con poco grado de razonamiento	vs.	La otra enseña el valor de la persistencia para buscar las relaciones matemáticas
Una forma enfatiza las destrezas de manera aislada y presenta las matemáticas como una serie de ideas discretas, separadas y sin relación	vs.	La otra enfatiza la interrelación de las ideas en las matemáticas y las destrezas que se crean en el contexto de su uso
Una forma tiene como resultado que muchos niños y adultos piensen que las matemáticas y en particular la multiplicación son algo que hay que temer y evitar	vs.	La otra enseña a los niños a amar las matemáticas y a fascinarse con los patrones que van descubriendo mediante su raíz
Una forma prepara a los niños poco menos que para competir con las calculadoras y como resultado, los adultos no son capaces de determinar si la información de la calculadora tiene sentido	vs.	La otra prepara a los niños a usar las matemáticas para encontrar sentido en las situaciones complejas de nuestro mundo tecnológico

Un enfoque tiene como resultado niños que pueden saber o no saber las tablas de multiplicar

vs.   El otro enfoque enseña . . .

Los textos de investigaciones usados en el taller

Math by All Means y *Teaching Arithmetic,* una serie para los grados 2–4 por Marilyn Burns. Estas unidades de muchas semanas enfocan en la geometría, el valor de la colocación, multiplicación, división, probabilidad, y el dinero.

A Collection of Math Lessons from Grades 3-6 por Marilyn Burns. Aquí se encuentran lecciones de multiplicación con rectángulos y patronas en las tablas de multiplicación.

Developing Number Concepts por Kathy Richardson. Esta serie de libros (y los recursos que siguen) enfocan en el desarrollamiento de la fluidez con los números.

Math Time: The Learning Environment por Kathy Richardson.

Mathematical Power: Lessons from a Classroom por Ruth Parker y el resultado de su año de investigadora en una clase del quinto grado. Enfoca en la necesidad por los cambios complejos en la enseñanza de las matemáticas y sigue a un maestro que intenta hacer los cambios.

Seeing Fractions por Susan Jo Russell y Rebecca Corwin. Esta unidad de 6–8 semanas de las fracciones es apropiada por los de los grados 4–6 y también ilustra lo que es un buen curículo para las matemáticas. Ahora, forma parte de la serie K–5 *Investigations in Number, Data, and Space.*

Why Numbers Count: Quantitative Literacy for Tomorrow's America por Lynn A. Steen. Este libro presenta la necesidad por los cambios en la manera en que los niños comprenden el número.

Otros Buenos Recursos de las Matemáticas para los Padres

About Teaching Mathematics por Marilyn Burns. Este libro es un recurso excelente que presenta problemas a través de las disciplinas de matemáticas.

Beyond Facts and Flashcards: Exploring Math with Your Kids por Jan Mokros. Este libro sugiere muchas maneras y prácticas diariamente para explorar matemáticas de familia.

Family Math por el Lawrence Hall of Science.

The I Hate Math Book y *Math for Smarty Pants,* los dos por Marilyn Burns y llenos de problemas divertidos para toda la familia.

Recursos Profesionales que Enfocan en los Asuntos de la Educación de Mathemáticas

On the Shoulders of Giants, editado por Lynn Arthur Steen.

Principles and Standards for School Mathematics por the Concilio Nacional de los Maestros de Matemáticas.

Thinking Mathematically por Leone Burton. Tiene el plan de interesarle a usted en pensarse a si mismo como una persona que puede resolver problemas.

El informe de la investigación

El Concilio Nacional de Investigaciones. (2001). *Adding it Up: Helping Children Learn Mathematics.* **J. Kilpatrick, J. Swafford, B. Findell (Eds.). Mathematics Learning Study Committee, Center for Education, División of Behavioral and Social Sciences and Education, Washington DC: National Academy Press. www.nap.edu**

Extractos: Este informe fue aprobado por la Junta Nacional del Concilio Nacional de Investigaciones, cuyos miembros son de los Concilios de la Academia Nacional de las Ciencias, la Academia Nacional de Ingeniería, y el Instituto de Medicina. Los miembros del comité responsables por el informe fueron elegidos por sus capacidades especiales con respeto al equilibrio apropiado. Estuvieron encargados de lo siguiente:

- sintetizar las ricas y diversas investigaciones de matemáticas desde el pre-kinder hasta el grado 8

- proveer recomendaciones basadas en las investigaciones por la enseñanza, la educación de los maestros, y el currículo con la intención de mejorar el aprendizaje estudiantil y de identificar áreas donde sea necesario más investigación

- aconsejar y guiar a los maestros, investigadores, publicadores, los encargados de establecer mandatos educativos, y los padres

Adding It Up presenta muchas preguntas: ¿Qué sabemos, precisamente, de la investigación de la enseñanza y el aprendizaje de matemáticas? ¿Qué presenta la investigación, en realidad? ¿Deben aprender las maneras de computación antes de comprender los conceptos básicos? ¿Cuál es el rol de los manipulativos? ¿Es verdad que las expectativas de los estudiantes y maestros hacen una diferencia? Las conclusiones y recomendaciones sacadas del reportaje de las investigaciones nos proveen con información concreta sobre el mejoramiento de la enseñanza y el aprendizaje de matemáticas.

Citas seleccionadas:

> Cuanto más conceptos de matemáticas que comprenden los estudiantes, lo más sentido tiene el estudio de matemáticas. Por el contrario, cuando los estudiantes raramente reciben problemas difíciles de resolver, vuelven a esperar que la memorización en vez del uso de la razón conduce al aprendizaje de matemáticas. (p. 131)

> Parece claro que la instrucción que enfoca solamente en la manipulación de los símbolos sin la comprensión no es efectiva para la mayoría de los estudiantes. Es necesario corregir el equilibrio equivocado tanto por prestar más atención a la comprensión conceptual como por los otros hilos de pericia y por ayudar a que los estudiantes puedan conectar con ellos. (p. 241)

> Al enfocarse en las maneras en que se puede utilizar los currículos de la escuela primaria y la mediana para apoyar el desarrollo del razonamiento algebráica, estos esfuerzos intentan evitar las dificultades que muchos estudiantes encuentran ahora y también proveen un fondo mejor para las matemáticas en la escuela secundaria. De los grados más jóvenes, los estudiantes pueden adquirir los básicos de álgebra, en particular con su aspecto representacional. (p. 280)

Mid-continent Research for Education and Learning. (2002). *EDThoughts, What We Know About Mathematics Teaching and Learning.* **J. Sutton & A. Krueger (Eds.).**

Extractos: Este libro resume las investigaciones y las encuestas de las mejores prácticas en la clase y ofrece implicaciones para mejorar el aprendizaje y la enseñanza. Responde a las cuestiones distintas relacionadas con la educación de matemáticas, provee un fondo para cada uno desde la perspectiva de las investigaciones y mejores prácticas seguidas por sugerencias para mejorar la enseñanza en la clase. No solo para los maestros y los administradores, sino también este libro reconoce que todos los que tienen interés en la enseñanza necesitarán un entendimiento común de la condición actual de la enseñanza y la dirección en que indican un mejoramiento las investigaciones y las mejores prácticas. "Cada persona que tiene interés en la enseñanza y el aprendizaje de matemáticas, que sea maestro, administrador, estudiante, padre o miembro de la comunidad, encontrará muy útil la información en este documento."

Resumen: ¿Qué sabemos de cómo aprenden los estudiantes las matemáticas?

Los estudiantes pueden tener dificultades haciendo la transición entre las aritméticas y el álgebra. Las investigaciones muestran como el desarrollo del razonamiento algebráica puede estar apoyado en la primaria y la mediana. Los jóvenes pueden aprender los conceptos de álgebra, especialmente la representación algebráica y las nociones de un variable y una función, y conceptos básicos pueden ser introducidos como modelos y como una generalización de las aritméticas. Por ejemplo, los modelos en una tabla de números de 100 puede estar descubierto y analizado. (p. 76)

Washington State Office of the Superintendent of Public Instruction. (2000). *Teaching and Learning Mathematics: Using Research to Shift From the "Yesterday" Mind to the "Tomorrow" Mind.* **J. Johnson (Ed.).**

Extractos: Este libro provee una vista general de la potencial y los desafíos de enseñar con calidad las matemáticas (K–12). La mayor parte resume algunos de los resultados de las investigaciones, de una manera concisa, relacioncionada a cada uno de los requisitos académicos y esenciales en el aprendizaje de matemáticas. Es un texto de recursos con el propósito de promover reflección, discusión, y el resolver los problemas dentro de la comunidad educativa, y ayudar a los maestros a conocer los resultados y las maneras en que pueden integrarlos en la clase. Se puede conseguir a www.k12.wa.us

Resumen

Los estudiantes que aprenden multiplicación como una función conceptual necesitan ver una variedad de modelos (ej: una area de varios rectángulos). El acceso a "los modelos de la multiplicación como una repetición de sumar" conduce a unas equivocaciones básicas de la multiplicación que podrán complicar las percepciones en el futuro cuando hay multiplicación de décimos y fracciones. (Bell, Greer, Mangan, y Grimison; y English y Halford, p. 9)

Resumen

El uso de materiales concretos dentro del contexto de matemáticas por los estudiantes ayuda tanto en las primeras construcciones de conceptos correctos y procesos como en el recuerdo y la habilidad de corregirse en estos conceptos y procesos por imágenes mentales. (Fuson, p. 43)

Referencias

Bell, A., Greer, B., Mangan, C., y Grimison, L. "Children's Performance on Multiplicative Word Problems: Elements of a Descriptive Theory." *Journal for Research In Mathematics Education,* 1989, 20(5): 434-449.

Fuson, K. "Mathematics Education, Elementary." In M. Alkin (Ed.) *Encyclopedia of Educational Research* (Sixth Ed, Vol. 3). New York: MacMillan, 1992c.

Documento de Reaprovechamiento

El título del taller: _____

Sitio: _____ Fecha: _____

1. ¿Qué ideas nuevas tiene usted después de este taller?

2. ¿Qué ideas de este taller va usted a usar con los niños?

3. En general, ¿cómo calificará usted este taller?

No aprendí   Aprendí   Aprendí
mucho   bastante   muchísimo

4. ¿Hay algo más, en su opinión, que debemos saber?

5. ¿Quisiera usted saber de los talleres en el futuro? Si lo quiere, por favor, dénos la siguiente información:

Nombre: _____

Domicilio: _____

_____

_____

Su Correo Electrónico: _____